MECHANIZED JUGGERNAUT OR MILITARY ANACHRONISM?

The Stackpole Military History Series

THE AMERICAN CIVIL WAR

Cavalry Raids of the Civil War
Ghost, Thunderbolt, and Wizard
Pickett's Charge
Witness to Gettysburg

WORLD WAR II

Armor Battles of the Waffen-SS, 1943–45
Army of the West
Australian Commandos
The B-24 in China
Backwater War
The Battle of Sicily
Beyond the Beachhead
The Brandenburger Commandos
The Brigade
Bringing the Thunder
Coast Watching in World War II
Colossal Cracks
A Dangerous Assignment
D-Day to Berlin
Dive Bomber!
A Drop Too Many
Eagles of the Third Reich
Exit Rommel
Fist from the Sky
Flying American Combat Aircraft of World
   War II
Forging the Thunderbolt
Fortress France
The German Defeat in the East, 1944–45
German Order of Battle, Vol. 1
German Order of Battle, Vol. 2
German Order of Battle, Vol. 3
The Germans in Normandy
Germany's Panzer Arm in World War II
GI Ingenuity
The Great Ships
Grenadiers
Infantry Aces
Iron Arm
Iron Knights
Kampfgruppe Peiper at the Battle
   of the Bulge
Kursk
Luftwaffe Aces
Massacre at Tobruk

Mechanized Juggernaut or Military
   Anachronism?
Messerschmitts over Sicily
Michael Wittmann, Vol. 1
Michael Wittmann, Vol. 2
Mountain Warriors
The Nazi Rocketeers
On the Canal
Operation Mercury
Packs On!
Panzer Aces
Panzer Aces II
Panzer Commanders of the Western Front
The Panzer Legions
Panzers in Winter
The Path to Blitzkrieg
Retreat to the Reich
Rommel's Desert Commanders
Rommel's Desert War
The Savage Sky
A Soldier in the Cockpit
Soviet Blitzkrieg
Stalin's Keys to Victory
Surviving Bataan and Beyond
T-34 in Action
Tigers in the Mud
The 12th SS, Vol. 1
The 12th SS, Vol. 2
The War against Rommel's Supply Lines
War in the Aegean

THE COLD WAR / VIETNAM

Cyclops in the Jungle
Flying American Combat Aircraft:
   The Cold War
Here There Are Tigers
Land with No Sun
Street without Joy
Through the Valley

WARS OF THE MIDDLE EAST

Never-Ending Conflict

GENERAL MILITARY HISTORY

Carriers in Combat
Desert Battles
Guerrilla Warfare

MECHANIZED JUGGERNAUT OR MILITARY ANACHRONISM?

Horses and the German Army
of World War II

R. L. DiNardo

STACKPOLE
BOOKS

Published in paperback in 2008 by
STACKPOLE BOOKS
5067 Ritter Road
Mechanicsburg, PA 17055
www.stackpolebooks.com

Cover design by Tracy Patterson
Cover photo courtesy of Scott Pick/Summit Photographics

Printed in the United States of America

10 9 8 7 6 5 4 3 2 1

ISBN 0-8117-3503-6 (Stackpole paperback)
ISBN 978-0-8117-3503-2 (Stackpole paperback)

Library of Congress Cataloging-in-Publication Data

DiNardo, R. L.
    Mechanized juggernaut or military anachronism? : horses and the German Army of World War II / R.L. DiNardo ; foreword by Williamson Murray.
        p. cm.
    Originally published: New York : Greenwood Press, 1991.
    Includes bibliographical references and index.
    ISBN-13: 978-0-8117-3503-2
    ISBN-10: 0-8117-3503-6
    1. World War, 1939–1945—Transportation—Germany. 2. World War, 1939–1945—Cavalry operations. 3. Germany. Heer—Transportation. 4. Germany. Heer—Cavalry—History. 5. Horses—Germany—History—20th century. I. Title.
    D810.T8D56 2008
    940.54'1343—dc22
                                        2008011734

TO CYNTHIA, WHO NEVER LOST FAITH

Contents

Photographs follow page 70.

Maps

Foreword

Richard DiNardo has provided us with a fine study on how dependent the German Army was on the horse during World War II. One of the current trends in modern military history has been to single out the Germans for their brilliant and innovative approach to war. That view has consistently argued that the Germans have provided a paradigm upon which all military organizations should model themselves. The reality is in fact somewhat different. While the German Army was capable of training and preparing soldiers for the sharp end of conflict in an extraordinary fashion, it did have several substantial weaknesses. Some of its difficulties were induced by the geographic and strategic weaknesses inherent in the Third Reich's position on the Continent, but many of these were self induced and for the most part remained unrecognized by the German military structure.

In effect, the German Army in 1939 and for the remainder of the war was one of the least modern engaged on the battlefields of Europe. For a variety of reasons, the 1930s caught German society in the midst of the process of motorization, a process that placed it well behind what was happening in the United States. And that state of affairs was reflected in the preparation of the German Army for war. No matter how skillful the leadership of the German Army was in operational art and on the battlefield, combat competence could not make up for the fact that the great bulk of the army marched to war with its equipment drawn by horses. The disparity between the armored, motorized élite and the regular, plodding infantry became more glaring as the war continued. No level of military competence could bridge that gap.

Richard DiNardo has, consequently, rendered us an immense service in recounting the problems involved in managing the horse-drawn side of the German Army. It is a tale that has needed telling, and it makes clear that the German Army of 1939 was not ten feet tall.

Professor Williamson Murray
The Ohio State University

Acknowledgments

A book is rarely the accomplishment of one person, and this one is no exception. The research for this book could never have been completed without the help of the following people: Special thanks go to Dr. George Wagner of the National Archives, whose encyclopedic knowledge of the German Army was invaluable. After Dr. Wagner retired, his successor, Mr. Harry Rilley, took a strong interest in the book and helped especially with locating naval documents relating to the Norwegian campaign. It was through the efforts of Major Peter Henry and Captain Keith Bonn of the U.S. Army, Colonel Doctor Roland Forster and Colonel Doctor Manfred Kehrig of the Militärgechichtlichen Forschungsamt and the Bundesarchiv-Militärarchiv, respectively, that I was able to obtain selected documents from Germany. Many thanks, also, to Dr. Richard Sommers and the staff of the U.S. Army War College in Carlisle, Pennsylvania, for their assistance in going through all of the manuscript material located in its archives. I am also indebted to the library staff at the U.S. Military Academy at West Point for their help to me in conducting my research.

I would also like to thank a number of other people who greatly helped me in completing this book. Professor Williamson Murray provided me with a number of useful comments and suggestions and very kindly took time out from his own hectic schedule to write the Foreword to this volume. Professor Sir Michael Howard also very kindly discussed the project with me and contributed some of his own experiences in Italy during World War II. Professor Jurgen Rohwer responded to my questions about the Norwegian campaign and the projected invasion of England. Professor Daniel Penham also ren-

dered valuable assistance in helping me go through some of
the documentation from the Bundesarchiv-Militärarchiv. Professor Brian Sullivan also provided many perceptive comments, as well as much interesting information on the Italian
Army. Thanks also to Dr. Samuel Mitcham, Jr., who very gra-
ciously gave of his time and photographic equipment at the
Photographic Archives of the Army War College to shoot some
of the photos included in this book. I would also like to
express my gratitude to my colleagues and students at Saint
Peter's College for their constant support. Saint Peter's provided some needed financial support for several research trips.
Finally, special thanks must go to my dear friends Scott Rosen-
thal and Mary Hansen, whose hospitality turned many a potentially dreary research trip to Washington, D.C., into very
enjoyable experiences.

I would also like to thank all those people who gave me
their constant support in this project: Sheila Rabin, Irving Kel-
ter, Janice Gordon-Kelter, Carl Slater, Ellen Hassman, Albert
Nofi, Jay Stone, Kathy Williams, Andrea Martin, Martin McDow-
ell, Valerie Eads, and Marita Boes. Special thanks also to Vivian
Penham. I would also like to acknowledge the contribution of a
former student of mine, Anna Demaras, whose expert knowledge of horses proved invaluable to me when I first embarked
on this book years ago. Most of all, I would like to thank my
parents and family for putting up with me through all of this.

An author's first scholarly book is the result not only of his
or her own research but also of the education received in both
undergraduate and graduate school. Therefore, I would like to
thank my undergraduate and graduate professors for the
excellent education they provided me. In particular, I would
like to mention Professor Cynthia Whittaker of Baruch College, who throughout my academic career has been my
teacher and mentor, and who is now a close friend. It is in gratitude that I dedicate this book to her.

Although many people have been mentioned here, all of
the work presented in this book is my own. I freely accept
responsibility for all errors and omissions.

Introduction

Along with the columns of vehicles carrying Nazi digni-
taries there came armored vehicles and motorized units
with their serried ranks of Panzers and other fighting
vehicles. These were glittering affairs, yet behind the
glamor lurked problems, some of which were due to
mistaken policies, but others to difficulties so funda-
mental as to render the entire course on which the
Wehrmacht was now embarked highly questionable.

Martin van Creveld[1]

No twentieth-century military machine has generated a
greater corpus of literature than the German Army of
World War II. A vast number of studies have been published
dealing with the activities of the General Staff and its relationship with Adolf Hitler. There have also been numerous studies
of the various campaigns and of a few of the various branches
of the army, with major attention devoted to the panzer arm.
There are also an enormous number of memoirs, which we
shall have course to discuss later in this book.

All of this printed matter, whatever its value (or lack
thereof), has left us, however, with a somewhat distorted
notion of the German Army. This distortion is reinforced by
the image of the German Army that has come down to us
through war and newsreel footage, as well as documentaries
such as the acclaimed BBC production, *The World at War.* Consequently, one of the great misconceptions of World War II is
the notion that the German Army was some sort of mechanized juggernaut—to use Frank Capra's term—the epitome of

mechanical efficiency, combining lightning speed and awesome military power.

To some degree, of course, this was true. The German panzer divisions were formidable units, élite by anyone's standard. Yet it is important to remember that these units, including the motorized infantry (later redesignated panzer grenadier) divisions and their SS counterparts, generally composed well under 25 percent of the divisions deployed by the German Wehrmacht.[2] The majority of the other divisions consisted of marching infantry. For transportation, these divisions had to depend largely on what commanders from Alexander the Great through Moltke the Younger had relied, namely the horse.

The study of the German Army's use of horses is in itself an interesting and important matter.[3] Indeed, I will present an extended examination of this question. Yet, the use of horses is also symptomatic of a broader issue dealing with the German Army, that of modernization. How modern was the German Army? Could the German Army have achieved a greater level of modernity than it actually did? Here the matter of the German economy's ability (or inability) to equip the German Army, as well as its operation under the Nazi regime, comes into question.

Part of this book will also address the mindset of the German Army. Were its plans and operations devised in conformity with its capabilities and limitations? Did this change as the war went on and as Germany's position deteriorated?

In dealing with horses specifically, we must seek answers to the following questions: How extensive was the German Army's dependence on horses? Was the decision to depend on horses a conscious one? Did it have an effect on the army's organization, or, to use modern parlance, on force structure? How did the use of horses affect the army in its conduct of operations? What problems arising from the use of horses did the Germans encounter? I will try to answer these questions as thoroughly as the available documentation will allow.

One matter that I will discuss only tangentially here will be agriculture. Horses were still the major source of tractive power on European farms during the World War II era. Thus a substantial use of horses could have an effect on agriculture, as was certainly the case in Germany during World War I when the overmobilization of horses for military needs damaged German agriculture.[4] Yet, I will offer no extended analysis of this matter. This is first and foremost a work of military history; matters such as the state of European agriculture during World War II are best left to economic historians infinitely more qualified than myself to discuss such topics.

CHAPTER 1

Wishes and Reality: The German Army, 1933–1939

That's what I need! That's what I want to have!

Adolf Hitler, 1933[1]

Therefore, it is not justifiable under the present circumstances, that the horse's service not be made use of.

Anonymous, 1937[2]

Like all the other armies of World War I, the major mode of transport in the German Army was, after the railroad, the horse. In fact, the single item most in demand in logistical terms during World War I was fodder for horses.[3] During the 1920s, however, the German Army began its experiments with motor vehicles. Spearheaded by the activities of Heinz Guderian, Oswald Lutz, and Erich von Tsischwitz, these experiments would eventually culminate in the creation of the panzer arm.[4] In many ways, however, the German Army was still hamstrung by the Versailles Treaty. The military clauses of the treaty denied the German Army tanks, aircraft, heavy artillery, and any other type of weapon thought to be useful for offensive purposes. The German Army, led by the chief of the General Staff, General Hans von Seekt, naturally sought to and did partially circumvent these restrictions.[5] Nonetheless, by the time Hitler took office as chancellor in January 1933, the German Army could not be considered either large or well armed. This was a situation that Hitler was determined to alter.

Hitler could certainly be described as cunning, devious, and deceitful in his pronouncements on a great many issues, especially in foreign policy. On one matter, however, he had

1

always been crystal clear, and that was the Versailles Treaty, including its military clauses. He made no secret of his ardent desire to tear up the treaty and restore Germany's military strength. This was made quite clear in *Mein Kampf* when he declared that "the aim of a German foreign policy of today must be the preparation for the reconquest of freedom for tomorrow."[6] That, along with his declared notions of eastern expansion, clearly showed that Germany's army would be expanded in the event of Hitler's coming to power. Now that it had occurred, just what kind of army would Germany develop?

In terms of land warfare, Hitler was always attracted to what were, at that time, considered novel forms of warfare, such as the mass employment of motorized troops and tanks, hence his excited statement to General Guderian at being shown them for the first time. In fact, the support of Hitler was absolutely vital to the successful development of the panzer arm.[7] Yet his misunderstanding of the equipment needs of a large motorized or armored force, as well as his disagreement with the successor to von Seekt as chief of the General Staff, General Ludwig Beck, over the pace of rearmament, led to the creation of a force that is described by Martin van Creveld as "semi-motorized."[8] A slightly more accurate description might be semimodern.

For a country to arm and maintain a large armored or motorized force in the field, several prerequisites must be achieved. Since these units rely primarily on vehicles, a country must have a well-developed motor vehicle industry to produce them in requisite numbers. A large tractor industry is helpful for producing tracked or half-tracked vehicles. An obvious corollary to this would be a substantial oil refining industry, as well as a secure oil source, without which vehicles are useless. Another important item here is an efficient maintenance service for repairing damaged vehicles. Combat vehicles also require several kinds of highly sophisticated equipment. This would include electrical wiring, communications, and optics.

According to the famed military historian B. H. Liddell-Hart, there are some twenty basic raw materials vital to the waging of war. These include oil, coal, iron, rubber, lead, copper, and aluminum, to name a few.[9] In almost all of these, Germany was deficient. For our purposes, however, we shall concentrate only on the two most important materials involved in the production and use of tanks and motor vehicles, namely steel and oil.

Right from the start, Germany's position in steel production was precarious. Germany was one of the major steel producers of Europe, but was lacking an indigenous supply of iron ore. Although strenuous attempts were made by *Reichsmarschall* Hermann Göring's Four Year Plan to increase iron ore production, these were opposed by German steel industries, who considered the extraction of low-grade German iron ore a process both too expensive and impractical.[10] In fact, both before and during the war, Germany received most of its iron ore from Sweden, reaching a high of 10.3 million tons in 1943.[11] During the prewar period, fairly substantial amounts of iron ore were also imported from the Soviet Union and southeastern Europe.[12] Given these circumstances, Germany entered her period of rearmament and later the war poorly prepared.

Germany's position with regard to oil was also very weak. In 1933 Germany produced 233,000 tons of crude oil.[13] This was minor compared with Romania's production of 7,377,000 tons and the Soviet Union's output of 21,489,000 tons.[14] Matters were not improved by Hitler's contradictory desires in this area. He clearly wanted Germany to become self-sufficient in oil and to become a fully motorized economy, but projects such as the autobahns and the mass production of the Volkswagen served only to increase oil consumption and hence Germany's dependence on imported oil.[15] This dependence was already marked. As early as 1934, for example, Germany consumed about three million tons of petroleum products, of which 85 percent were imported.[16] The Austrian Anschluss did little to improve this situation, although it did provide Germany with an extra indigenous source of iron ore.[17]

If Germany did have one advantage, it was in its ability to produce synthetic oil. Germany built the first synthetic oil plant after World War I. The synthetic oil program was supported by the military, but the only company to express interest in the rather expensive process was I. G. Farben. The Depression almost destroyed the synthetic oil program when it created an oil glut. Its survival and expansion, however, were assured by Hitler's coming to power.[18] Although ahead of the rest of the world in this area, synthetic oil production as late as 1938 amounted to only 1.6 million tons.[19]

Germany's ability to produce the requisite equipment for a motorized army was also limited by several other factors. Among these was the question of who was responsible for the direction of the process of rearmament, not to mention the economy as a whole. Hitler himself never provided any clear direction in this, as he had only a limited interest in general economic matters, a situation that continued into the war.[20] Initially, the authority for rearmament rested with two agencies, the Wehrmacht's Office of Economics and Armaments (*Wirtschafts und Rüstungs Amt*, or *Wi Rü Amt*), headed by Major General Georg Thomas, and the Reich Ministry of Economics (*Reichswirtschaftsministerium*, or *RWM*), headed by Dr. Hjalmar Schacht.

Then in 1936 Hitler, ostensibly for the purpose of preparing for war, created the "Four Year Plan" and placed the agency under Göring. This was a poor decision in two ways. First, although Hitler chose Göring for his "energy," the *Reichsmarschall* knew nothing about economics, and openly said so.[21] To be absolutely fair, however, it should be pointed out that Göring tried to surround himself with competent technical assistance to compensate for his own inadequacy in this area.[22]

The choice of Göring also did not bode well for the army or the navy, as he was both minister of aviation and commander of the Luftwaffe, and thus could be expected to starve the other two services of resources in favor of his own. After the outbreak of war, Hitler added yet another agency by creating the Ministry of Armaments and Munitions under Dr. Fritz Todt in 1940. In February 1942 Albert Speer succeeded Todt when the latter was killed in a plane crash.

The structure of the economy had several unfortunate effects, the primary of which was the question of who actually

ran the economy. Göring stated after the war that he and
Schacht encountered jurisdictional problems almost immediately after Göring's appointment.[23] The Armed Forces High
Command (OKW) was also not pleased, as their economic
staff (later *Wi Rü Amt*) strenuously opposed Göring's appointment.[24] To make matters worse, there was not even a strong
regulating mechanism among the armed services themselves.
Thus, the services competed not only against the civilian economy but against one another as well. Although Speer succeeded in imposing some order on this chaos in 1943, it was
far too late to affect either the nature of the German Army or
the outcome of the war.

In this rather general discussion of why Germany's economy could not produce equipment in amounts needed to create a motorized, modern army, another question does come
up. Should Germany have built a navy? One aspect of this in
particular would be the construction of large surface units,
such as the pocket battleships, the cruisers *Scharnhorst* and
Gneisenau, and especially the capital ships *Bismarck* and *Tirpitz*.

Given Germany's position as a continental power and the
realities of twentieth-century warfare, Germany's need for an
air force as part of its overall rearmaments scheme was quite
clear. A large surface fleet, however, is another matter. It rep-
resents a large investment in time, money, and resources.
Exactly what role a large surface navy could play in German
foreign policy was unclear, especially given Hitler's continental
aspirations. Also, German naval construction was limited by
the Anglo-German Naval Agreement of 1935.

In 1937, however, naval construction resumed at full tilt.
In the ensuing scramble for resources, Grand Admiral Erich
Raeder was able to obtain, at the 5 November 1937 conference, a monthly steel allocation of 74,000 tons.[25] To the army,
this was the potential for a great many more tanks, trucks, and
guns. Yet, they went to a service that could not be ready for
war until 1944, at the earliest.[26]

The German automobile industry was another reason
behind the failure of the Nazi regime to create a modern,

motorized German Army. To be effective, divisions, panzer or otherwise, need to be supported by a variety of vehicles, the most important of which are the trucks needed to tow artillery and to carry gasoline, ammunition, and men. Yet it is quite clear that Germany's automobile industry was not up to the task of producing the requisite number of vehicles needed to give Germany a completely motorized army.

Speer believed that Germany's automobile industry was working up to modern standards of efficiency when he took up his duties in February 1942.[27] In fact, however, the German automobile industry was poorly suited to meet Germany's needs in either modernizing its army or fighting a war, and was underutilized in both cases. There was apparently no system in place by 1939 for converting the automobile industry to war production, and even as late as 1944, the army was still using large numbers of civilian trucks, which were quite unsuited to military service.[28] Since the German motor vehicle industry was incapable of satisfying Germany's needs, the Germans had to resort to the risky expedient of using captured equipment, about which more will be said later.

Another area that contributed to the lack of modernization of the German Army was the German population. One of the most important prerequisites for the creation of a large armored or motorized force is an automotively inclined population, that is, a population that has extensive contact with automobiles, trucks, or any other automotive devices. Perhaps the best way to measure such an inclination in a population is to look at the number of people per vehicle in a country. By this measurement, Germany was in a very backward state automotively. Guderian, in a 1935 article, stated that in 1933 there was one vehicle for every five people in the United States, while in Germany there was one vehicle for every seventy-five people.[29] In fact, things were even worse than Guderian stated. In 1933 the ratio was actually one vehicle for every eighty-nine people. Although strenuous efforts reduced this ratio by 1937 to one vehicle for every forty-seven people, it was still the poorest ratio in Western Europe, with the exception of Italy.[30] Thus,

Germany did not have a population conducive to the creation of a large motorized or mechanized force.

The Nazi regime tried to remedy this problem through the use of National Sozialist Deutsche Arbeits Partei (NSDAP) organizations, most notably the Hitler Youth and the National Socialist Motorized Corps (NSKK). The Hitler Youth itself was not a homogeneous organization but was divided into flying units, naval units, and so on.[31] For the army, the Hitler Youth Motorized Units were the most important element of the Hitler Youth. The motorized Hitler Youth expanded from 3,000 members in 1933 to 102,000 in 1938. Training in this organization included both driving and mechanics. A member was generally given 80 hours of driving time and 105 hours of mechanical training. This was clearly intended as preparation for service in the Wehrmacht.[32]

Once a member of the Hitler Youth passed out of the organization, the NSKK took over his training. Between 1933 and 1939 the NSKK trained 187,000 drivers for the army.[33] The NSKK also trained personnel for maintenance shops and repair units. Certainly this training would influence the final determination as to a soldier's branch of service. Despite these efforts, however, the German Army remained eternally short of drivers and personnel for salvage and maintenance units.

The army's effort at modernization was also impaired by the breakneck pace of its expansion. The army leaders, Beck in particular, wanted the army to expand at a much slower pace for several reasons. First, Beck was deeply worried about the implications for Germany's foreign relations as a result of an overly rapid expansion of the army. In fact, one can interpret Beck's opposition to Hitler's designs for a thirty-six-division army as an attack on the principles of Hitler's foreign policy.[34] Second, Beck realized that the faster pace of rearmament was beyond the capabilities of the German economy. Beck argued that a smaller army would have a higher degree of motorization. Beck's ideal concept of what he called an "attack army" consisted of a motorized army built around a core of armored units.[35]

In the end, however, the faster pace of rearmament demanded by Hitler was adopted, although Beck and the commander-in-chief of the army, Colonel General Werner von Fritsch, were able to moderate it somewhat.[36]

In summary, it is clearly evident that the German economy was incapable of providing the vehicles and fuel requisite to the creation of a modern, fully motorized force. This was further exacerbated by the German population's relative unfamiliarity with motor vehicles and the breakneck pace of the army's expansion. Given these circumstances, horses had to be used for transportation, despite Hitler's supposed aversion to them.[37]

Before embarking on the main subject of this book, we must take a brief look at horses in general. This is necessary because in our automobile-dominated age, most people have little, if any, contact with horses. Horses come in many different breeds, but there are there main types—warm bloods, cold bloods, and mixed bloods.

Warm bloods vary in size and are characterized by rather lively and excitable temperaments. Spirited warm bloods make excellent riding horses. A fine example of a warm blood would be an Arabian horse, or an American thoroughbred race horse.

Cold bloods are the descendants of the Great Horses of medieval times.[38] These animals had once served as mounts for knights, but with the passing of the Middle Ages, they became draft horses. Given that role, cold bloods have always been bred for size and strength. They are also characterized by a rather docile temperament, from which the term "cold blood" is derived. A Clydesdale would be a good example of a cold blood.

Mixed bloods are the result of cross-breeding. They do not figure prominently in our story, but, as we shall see later, the Germans would conduct experiments with the aim of breeding a certain type of mixed blood.

All horses, whatever their breed, do share certain characteristics. The prime of these is a big appetite. Horses require an enormous amount of food. Even the hardiest horses need about twelve pounds of food per day. Larger horses proportionately require more food and water. A large cold blood can consume up to twenty pounds of food daily. In the absence of feed, horses can obtain sustenance by grazing on grass, but this would require about eight hours daily.[39]

Horses can eat a wide range of foods. In the German Army, horse fodder consisted of a combination of oats, hay, and straw, with oats considered to be the best.[40] A riding horse can develop speed by being fed corn constantly, as the Duke of Wellington did in the peninsula campaigns. His special reconnaissance service consisted of officers riding corn-fed mounts, who could almost always outrun the grain-fed French cavalry mounts.[41] When grazing, horses generally prefer grass but will also eat roots and even aquatic plants.[42]

Horses have sleeping habits as well. Most horses tend to sleep at night.[43] They can, however, be made to change their sleeping habits, just as human beings can. This was to prove valuable to the Germans in Normandy, when overwhelming Allied air power confined the German Seventh Army to making moves only at night.

For all their imposing size and physical appearance, horses are surprisingly delicate creatures. They are subject to a wide variety of diseases, some of which are highly contagious. For the purposes of this book, the most common maladies are mange, pneumonia, frostbite, and glanders. Of these ailments mange is the most common. Mange is a skin disease caused by mites or ticks that burrow under a horse's skin. Although a minor disease, it can become serious if left unchecked. Since the disease is tick-borne, it is also highly contagious. There are five types of mange, namely poultry mange, autumn mange, foot mange, sarcoptic mange, and psoroptic mange.[44] The disease is easily treatable with sulphur dioxide. Nonetheless, it would constitute the most common illness faced by German veterinary units.

Equine pneumonia is somewhat rarer but more serious. Pneumonia acts in horses the same way it acts in humans. It too is treatable with drugs, but horses suffering from pneumonia require a long period of convalescence, often extending into months. Putting a horse back to work before its recovery is complete often results in a fatal relapse.[45]

Like people, horses can also suffer from frostbite in extreme cold. This too is treatable but, again, requires an extended period of recovery that, like pneumonia, can last for several months.

Of all the diseases considered here, glanders is far and away the most serious. A germ-borne disease, it attacks a horse's respiratory system and is almost invariably fatal. Given the state of veterinary medicine in the 1930s and 1940s, there was no real cure. Rather, preventative measures had to be taken. The most important measure was disinfecting stables before quartering horses in them.[46]

Three other facts about horses are of interest here. First, a mare's gestation period is about eleven months. Second, a horse is incapable of work for about the first five years of its life. Finally, in the 1930s and 1940s horses still provided the tractive power on European farms. Thus, unless the obtaining of replacements was handled very carefully, a country's agriculture could be very severely affected by a shortage of horses.

Now that we have completed our brief general examination of horses, let us look at how the German Army used them. Given that the use of horses by the German Army was really mandated by the considerations discussed earlier, the question of sources now comes into play. If the German Army was to employ horses on a mass scale, and it surely would, given Hitler's desire for a large army, where would they come from? Foreign purchases provided some. When the British Army became a completely motorized force during the 1930s, the Germans bought up its stock of horses.[47] Hungary was also a source of horseflesh. As preparation for the army's expansion in 1935, the army purchased in the previous year at least twenty-five thousand horses from Hungary, spending up to ten million *Reichmarks* for them.[48] An interesting result of this was that the Germans cut the Italians out of the Hungarian horse market, later forcing Italian peasant farmers to return to the ox as the standard draft animal.

The major source of horses for the German Army was, however, Germany itself. This required an elaborate and complex organization that had to balance the needs of the army against those of the economy. Here, of course, the army worked very closely with the NSDAP. Proper military authorities in each military district (*Wehrkreise*) worked with party agricultural organizations to draw up lists of horses for every district in Germany.[49] Every horse was supposed to be registered and given a registration number (*Nummerriemen*), which was kept on an index card. The card also contained information such as the horse's name, age, description, and important medical information.[50] Thus, the German Army was, theoretically at least, well aware of the number of horses available for any particular year. This was especially important in the formulation of the annual remount plan.

Every year the German Army or, more specifically, the Inspectorate of Cavalry of the Army High Command (OKH), formulated a remount plan. The remount plan began with the army's individual units, which would submit requests for remounts early in the year. Newly formed divisions would request their authorized complement of animals. Units also had to submit at this time separate requests for special animals. These would include, for example, a mount for an especially tall or heavy officer, or a horse to carry kettle drums for a parade or other ceremonial occasions.[51] Branch schools also had to submit requests for remounts at this time. These requests would then percolate up through proper channels to the Inspectorate of Cavalry.

The Inspectorate of Cavalry was the section of OKH that had the final word on all equine matters. In 1938, however, the Inspectorate of Cavalry was replaced by the Inspectorate of Riding and Driving. This organization was responsible for horse breeding, procurement, distribution, management, remounts, registration, and training.[52] This was undoubtedly done because by this time the German Army used far more horses for draft work than for riding. Having received the requests from the units, the Inspectorate, be it of Cavalry or of Riding and Driving, would then correlate them all and formulate a remount plan.

The remount plan generally determined the number and types of remounts needed by the various schools and units. The plan also stipulated the number of horses to be sent to remount schools for training.[53]

The actual purchasing of horses for the army was carried out by the remount commission. Each *Wehrkreis* had a standing remount commission, although in certain circumstances auxiliary commissions could be created on a temporary basis.[54]

A remount commission had two permanently occupied positions, namely chairman and administrative officer, responsible to the Inspectorate of Cavalry and later of Riding and Driving for their activities. The two assistant officers were drawn from units in the *Wehrkreis* and assigned on a rotating basis. All officers had to be from the artillery or cavalry. A veterinary officer was assigned from and responsible to the Veterinary Inspectorate of the General Army Office, and several enlisted men were attached to the commission as orderlies.[55]

Remount commissions purchased horses at specially organized remount markets. Here the commissions would purchase horses from farmers, breeding establishments, and other such institutions, usually at a price set by the government. Commissions were specifically instructed not to buy certain types of horses, including thoroughbreds, pregnant mares, studs, and horses younger than three years of age.[56] At these occasions, the army would also sell horses who, although still capable of working on farms, were no longer fit for military service. Once purchased, horses were to be moved to branch schools by remount transport squads.[57] Generally this system worked well, although occasionally the remount commissions bought precisely the types of horses they were enjoined not to purchase.[58]

Generally, the German Army liked to buy a horse at about three years of age. The horse would then be given training at a *Wehrkreis* remount school. This would include drill instruction for riding and driving. The training of horses for the artillery would undoubtedly include getting the horses accustomed to loud noises, such as the report of artillery being fired. The training of officer remounts generally took two years, while training for other remounts lasted for only one year.[59]

The German Army divided horses into two basic classifications: mounts and draft horses. Mounts were then divided into mounts for officers, cavalry- and infantry-mounted vehicles, and mounts for all other branches.

Draft horses were even further subdivided. There were three types of light draft horses, namely pole horses, middle and leading horses, and finally machine gun horses. Heavy draft horses were divided into those for artillery and those for all other branches. Finally, there were the "heaviest" draft horses, a relatively rare group of horses used to haul heavy artillery. There were also pack horses and mules, but these were used only by mountain divisions. All of these horses were warm bloods, with the exception of heavy draft horses for nonartillery branches and the extra-heavy draft horses.[60]   *Barbarossa*

Such extensive use of horses also required extensive numbers of men for their care and maintenance. All men involved in riding and driving horses were given elementary veterinary training which would allow them to deal with minor problems that might arise in the course of a march or a campaign.[61] A large number of veterinarians, as well as blacksmiths, also had to be drafted. This type of manpower was in plentiful supply, because Germany's population was far more familiar with horses than with motor vehicles. In fact, throughout the entire period under consideration here, the German Army never lacked either veterinarians or blacksmiths. It proved possible to draft and commission veterinarians directly into the army. It also was generally agreed that country veterinarians were the best.[62] Conversely, it is interesting to note that the policy of drafting civilian mechanics directly into tank and vehicle maintenance units proved a failure.[63]

Aside from providing remounts in an organized fashion, the army also had to plan for the immediate mobilization of horses to go along with the mobilization of manpower. As always, this was done by the army in cooperation with NSDAP agricultural organizations. This theoretically was not only supposed to provide the army with the horseflesh it needed, but also to prevent overmobilization.[64]

The German Army's reliance on horses clearly had an effect on its organization, or what would be called in modern parlance its "force structure." For one thing, its reliance on horses, along with the horses' being grouped together into corps-sized units for campaigns, were probably two of the factors that necessitated the creation of the panzer divisions. As noted previously, Beck certainly wanted a smaller but completely motorized force. Had his desires been fulfilled, the German Army may well have borne a strong resemblance to the U.S. Army of World War II. Any chance of this, however, was frustrated by Germany's economic incapacity and the extremely rushed nature of the army's expansion after 1935.

Given these circumstances, it would have been extremely wasteful for the Germans to spread their tanks among the large number of infantry divisions relying on horse-drawn transportation.

Equally wasteful would have been the policy of spreading panzer and motorized infantry divisions individually among the army. Logic dictated that these divisions, in order to maximize their striking power, concentrate by creating corps composed of two or three panzer or motorized infantry divisions. The Germans had considered this idea right from the inception of the panzer arm in 1935.[65] These units would prove decisive in the early campaigns of the war yet also created two very different armies, "one fast and mobile and the other slow and plodding."[66] While this dual nature did not become a major factor in Poland and France, as we shall see, it did play a big part in the ultimate failure of Operation Barbarossa.

Another interesting result of the German Army's use of horses was a theoretical debate concerning antitank units. A number of writers argued during the 1920s that antitank units should be motorized, because, in order to be effective, the antitank gun had to travel just as fast, if not faster, than the tanks it would be trying to stop.[67] As the expansion began, however, some argued that antitank units were better horse drawn, as the march rate of a horse-drawn antitank unit would correspond more closely to the marching capabilities of the rest of the units in an infantry division.[68] As it turned out, the advocates of speed won, and German antitank units were motorized throughout the period under consideration.

The German Army may also have profited from its lack of motorization in the relationship between its officers and men, especially at the lower levels. In the German Army junior officers were given great latitude and responsibility in dealing with the men under their command. This was designed to promote trust and confidence between officers and men, especially from the regimental level on down.[69] This goal may have been furthered by the lack of motorization. A correspondent for the *Royal United Service Institution Journal*, writing under the pseudonym "Eurollydon" argued that the lack of motorization was militarily a good thing for officers. Because of the relative absence of motor transportation, and hence personal mobility, officers had to spend more time with their men for "self-employment and recreation." This made for better regimental officers.[70]

The German Army profited greatly from the occupations of Austria and Czechoslovakia in several ways. The most important of these was the experience gained by the Germans in conducting moves over long distances using armored and motorized units on a large scale, without having to do so under the pressure of combat. The problems encountered by German armored and motorized units in accomplishing these missions have been thoroughly documented and analyzed by Williamson Murray and thus are not worth repeating here.[71]

These operations, however, also gave the German Army valuable experience in mobilizing and handling large numbers of horses in a short period of time. As with the motorized and panzer troops, a number of problems, including some major embarrassments, occurred, especially during the Austrian operation.

For the occupation of Austria, the German Army conscripted some 14,870 horses from southern Germany for the operation. These horses were processed through either Nuremberg or Regensburg. Of these, 3,660 were immediately conscripted and sent to units of the XIII Corps. The remaining 11,210 were obtained by horse procurement commissions working with district agricultural organizations.

The population did not exactly prove enthusiastic about the conscription of horses. Many peasants were unwilling to give up their better draft horses to the army. Instead they brought their older or broken-down horses for sale to the army. The XIII Corps after-action report on the operation also noted indignantly that there were even "attempts at profiteering."[72] Many horses had been poorly fed and sheltered during the winter and thus were not capable of long marches and were susceptible to colds. Only about 10 percent of the horses were thought by the procurement commissions to be fit for immediate service with the troops. The rapid nature of the mobilization was also thought to be a problem. Better horses from the area could have been obtained with a longer and more deliberate period of mobilization. Finally, the demobilization of horses after the operation was beset by confusion. Many horses had the same identification number, a problem that could only be rectified by better record-keeping procedures.

Six months after the Austrian Anschluss, the XIII Corps was again involved in an occupying operation. This time the XIII Corps would occupy part of Czechoslovakia, in accordance with the Munich agreement. The German Army learned more valuable lessons from the occupation of Czechoslovakia; one lesson in the handling and use of large amounts of captured equipment again illuminated the German Army's lack of modernity.

A considerable amount of materiel was captured in Czechoslovakia, including 810 tanks.[73] This materiel, however, was poorly handled. Each occupying division gathered equipment and shipped each piece to various ordinance offices in Germany. This proved to be a serious mistake, as all the writing on the equipment was Czech, which few Germans could read.[74] The Germans were again fortunate, however, in that it was still peacetime, and they were able to profit from their mistakes once again. Nonetheless, such large-scale dependence on captured equipment, including tanks and motor vehicles, did not bode well.

In the use of horses, the occupation of the Sudetenland went a good deal more smoothly than did the Austrian Anschluss. The primary reason was that substantially fewer horses were conscripted for the occupation of Czechoslovakia than for Austria. While some 14,870 horses were conscripted for the Anschluss, only some 4,539 horses were conscripted for the occupation of the Sudetenland. Thus, the Germans learned that horses as well as men could be overmobilized. Although many fewer horses were conscripted, the XIII Corps after-action report noted that these completely satisfied the requirements. Although the report noted that the civilian population understood the needs of the Wehrmacht, there were still cases of peasants not bringing their better horses, or bringing in stallions, knowing that they would not be bought. Nevertheless, the number of fit horses conscripted was much greater than in the occupation of Austria. Although some regiments reported that as many as 30 percent of the remounts received were unfit, this was still a great improvement. The only things that required marked improvement were horse shoeing and the procurement commissions. Resources for getting all of the horses shod proved insufficient. That could be solved by giving civilian blacksmiths a special course on shoeing army horses. Also, it was recommended that procurement commissions, especially the commanders and veterinarians, be given more training.[75]

The Germans had to deal with large amounts of captured Czech equipment after Hitler had the Wehrmacht occupy the rump Czech state on 15 March 1939. As noted previously, the captured equipment was not well handled. Little information seems to be at hand on treatment of captured horses. The only specific reference to them is that Czech officers were allowed to retain their personal mounts.[76] The German Army would be less generous in the future.

The experience gained by the German Army in the mobilization of horses during the occupations of Austria and Czechoslovakia put the army in good stead during the following year. From 1938 to 1939, the German Army was able to mobilize some 400,000 horses.[77] With the mobilization completed, Hitler was now ready to unleash the Wehrmacht on Europe.

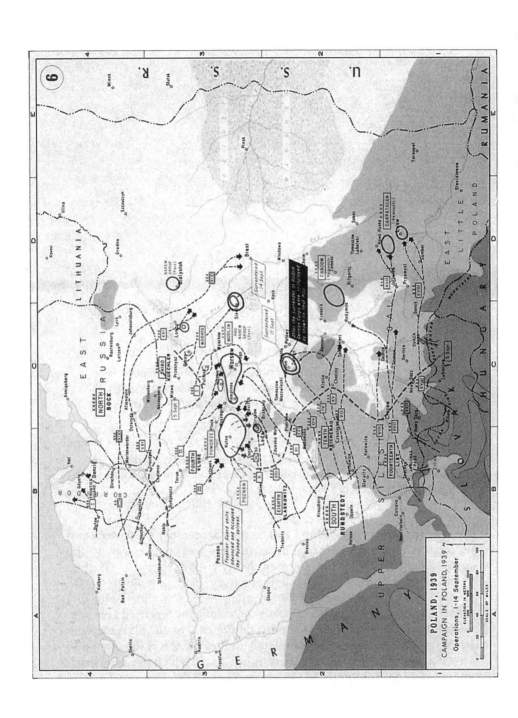

POLAND, 1939
CAMPAIGN IN POLAND, 1939
Operations, 1-14 September

CHAPTER 2

Blitzkrieg?

These measures then, would not solve our problem. They would have to be supplemented by a concurrent *demotorization program* on a big scale, which entails the procurement of horses, vehicles and harnesses.

Franz Halder, 4 February 1940[1]

The expression "Blitzkrieg" is an Italian invention. We picked it up from the newspapers. I've just learned that I owe all my successes to an attentive study of Italian military theories.

Adolf Hitler, 3 January 1942[2]

The German Army that entered Poland on 1 September 1939 was a curious mixture of old and new. The invasion force was composed of fifty-four divisions, roughly half of the German Army's total strength. Of these divisions, fourteen were mobile, that is, either panzer, light, or motorized infantry divisions. The rest were infantry, along with some mountain divisions.[3] All of the divisions facing the French along the Siegfried Line were second-line infantry and reserve units. Of the total of 102 divisions, only the 14 mobile divisions were completely motorized. All of the other divisions depended on varying numbers of horses, of which the Wehrmacht possessed some 590 thousand by 1 September 1939.[4]

The Polish campaign was a first in many ways for the German Army. It marked the debut of the expanded army in combat and also of German armored doctrine, developed during the interwar period by German theorists such as Guderian and Walter Nehring. Indeed, it was the image of German armored columns rampaging across the fiat Polish countryside that inspired a *Time* magazine correspondent to coin the term "Blitzkrieg."[5] The campaign also marked the first large-scale use of horses by the army since World War I.

From the point of view of the use of horses, the Polish campaign generally went well, although some problems were encountered. The Germans profited from the fact that the weather was dry, which minimized problems such as pneumonia. Strategically and tactically, the army also benefited from the complete command of the air enjoyed by the Luftwaffe from the very start of the campaign.

A complex organization was erected to deal with horses. Basically, when the Germany Army operated in the field, the following establishments were charged with the task of caring for and maintaining horses: three army horse hospitals, two army horse parks, and one veterinary examining station.6 The Tenth Army, for example, had for the care of its horses the 541st, 542nd, and 543rd Army Horse Hospitals, the 541st Army Horse Park, and the 540th Veterinary Park. In addition it had two blood examining stations.[7] At the lower level, each infantry division had its own divisional horse hospital, administered by the divisional veterinary company. There were apparently no veterinary units of any kind at corps level.

Theoretically, the flow of horses was to be carefully controlled. Basic care of the horses was left to the drivers and riders of the horses themselves. Horses requiring more serious medical care were to be sent back to the divisional horse hospital. To backup the divisional hospitals there were the army hospitals as well as the veterinary parks and examining stations. Horse parks were used to hold horses, who could then be passed on to divisions in need of replacements. A divisional horse hospital could care for about 500 horses, while an army horse hospital could handle about 550.[8]

Although the occupations of Austria and Czechoslovakia had given the Wehrmacht valuable experience in conducting large-scale movements, Poland was its first test in actual combat. While the end result was a triumph for German arms, a number of high-ranking officers were not entirely pleased with the German Army's performance. The infantry had not been "vigorous in the attack."[9] Even troops in the panzer and motorized units had gotten downright jittery at times.[10] March discipline also remained poor.

In terms of horses the campaign was generally an easy one, aided by cooperative weather and by German command of the air. That is not to say, however, that the campaign was problem-free. The 14th Infantry Division, for example, was still lacking veterinary equipment by 1 September 1939.[11] The 19th Infantry Division of the XI Corps was urgently requesting the dispatch of fifty replacement horses immediately, although the reason why was not specified.[12] As the campaign wore on, it became difficult to obtain replacements in Poland. Eventually, the troops were allowed to exchange horses for remounts from the Polish population.[13]

The handling of captured horses also presented problems. Initially, all captured horses were to be taken to horse hospitals for examination. These examinations were to check horses for symptoms of contagious diseases. They could then be sent either to Germany or to the army's horse parks. Eventually, however, the hospitals became clogged with more horses than they could handle.[14]

Aside from representing *Lebensraum* (living space) to Nazi ideologists, Poland also represented a source of valuable horseflesh. With an eye toward horse replacement in the latter stages of the campaign, troops were ordered to leave Polish breeding establishments, stud farms, and all similar establishments undisturbed.[15] The Wehrmacht's thinking here was not misplaced either, as Polish breeds eventually became one of the mainstays of the German Army's stock of horses.[16]

On 17 February 1940 the *Altmark*, the supply ship for the pocket battleship *Grafspee*, was captured and boarded by British Navy vessels in Norwegian territorial waters, and 300 British prisoners were set free. Hitler was convinced that the British would soon occupy Norway. Concerned about the security of Germany's access to supplies of Swedish iron ore following this incident, Hitler ordered the invasion of Norway on 21 February.[17] A mountainous country, Norway presented the German Army and Navy with serious problems. Since the terrain was rather ill suited to the employment of tanks in large numbers, the operation had to be carried out by infantry divisions. Germany's armed forces, and their Prussian antecedents, never had a tradition of conducting amphibious operations. Given that the infantry divisions depended on horses for transportation, the German faced the same difficulty as had the British for centuries. In fact, even with the vast shipping and naval resources at their disposal during the eighteenth and early nineteenth centuries, British amphibious operations had been consistently hamstrung by the inability to transport large numbers of horses.[18]

Given these circumstances, OKW put together a small ad hoc force under the command of General Nikolaus von Falkenhorst and gave it the rather pretentious title of Twenty-First Army, although it was later redesignated as XXI Army Corps. The force initially consisted of the 69th and 163rd Infantry Divisions, plus the 3rd Mountain Division. They would be followed by the 181st and 196th Infantry Divisions. A third wave, composed solely of the 214th Infantry Division, would be brought in later. Two infantry divisions, the 170th and 198th, along with the 11th Motorized Infantry Brigade, were allocated for the occupation of Denmark.[19]

Since the initial invasion was to be carried out by the 69th and 163rd Infantry Divisions and the 3rd Mountain Division, these divisions, as well as the first two follow-on infantry divisions, the 181st and 196th, had to be stripped down to the barest elements for sea transport. Only the essential combat units were to be sent. The leading troops would be carried on destroyers. Other troops and their equipment, along with horses, would be carried to Norwegian ports in merchant ships. The total number of horses carried in the first two waves amounted to no more than 1,691.[20] Since the average infantry division normally employed over 4,000 horses, this gives some indication as to how stripped down these divisions were.

The Norwegian campaign did provide the Germans with great strategic benefits, but at a tremendous cost. The small German surface navy suffered such severe losses as to be effectively emasculated for the rest of the war. Particularly serious were the losses of the cruiser *Blücher* and most of the German Navy's destroyers; by the end of the Norwegian campaign only ten were left.[21]

From the perspective of our subject, there are several points of interest. Both army and navy after-action reports on the campaign make extensive mention of the difficulties involved in transporting horses. The progress of the operation was greatly hindered when the merchant ship *Ionia*, part of the First Sea Transport Squadron carrying elements of the 69th and 163rd Infantry Divisions, bearing some 150 horses, was torpedoed by a British submarine on 11 April outside of Oslo. Attempts to save the ship failed, and it later capsized in Lavik Fjord. All of the horses were lost.[22] This represented 20 percent of the Oslo group's horse-drawn transportation.

The result was that the German artillery was severely restricted in its mobility. Not long after the onset of the operation, von Falkenhorst was making frantic telephone calls to Berlin for airpower, which he received. In fact, German airpower was certainly one of the deciding factors in the campaign.[23]

Even when the ships did get through, great problems were encountered. Much valuable time was lost in unloading horses from merchant ships, a complicated process requiring large amounts of equipment, including hoists, cranes, and crates. Also, the horses did not take well to the sea voyage, even one as short as this. Especially affected were the more delicate cold bloods, who showed stiffness and a need for fresh air after being confined in a narrow space. The condition of the horses rapidly improved, however, after they were unloaded. The losses in the first wave created transportation difficulties. The horses in the following waves arrived too late and did nothing but clog roads and consume supplies. The Twenty-First Army recommended that in the future an invading force should obtain its horses from indigenous sources.[24] Given these circumstances, the Wehrmacht's amphibious capability could be described as anything but formidable.

While Norway provided but a minor distraction for the army (for the navy it was a disaster), the Wehrmacht was preparing for its next major move, the invasion of France and the Low Countries. Despite the victory over Poland, Germany's economic position had deteriorated considerably. Petroleum fuel stocks of all types had declined to dangerously low levels by the winter of 1939/40.[25] Steel production declined from 22.5 million tons in 1939 to 19.1 million tons in 1940.[26] Given these alarming figures, Hitler argued with his military commanders that the only way to alleviate Germany's raw material position would be by conquering the west as quickly as possible.[27] Thus he wanted an invasion of the west to be mounted as early as November 1939.

While this was probably correct from a theoretical viewpoint, in reality the German Army was fortunate that it did not have to undertake an offensive against France and the Low Countries during the winter of 1939/40. Not only did the army require a period of strenuous training to correct the deficiencies that manifested themselves in Poland, but the logistics for such an offensive would have been nightmarish. In particular, a major problem would have been trying to maintain the health and strength of thousands of horses while conducting an offensive during what turned out to be an extraordinarily cold winter.

Ultimately, however, owing to bad weather, an egregious breach of security, and the need to build up fuel reserves, the offensive was postponed until the spring of 1940. The most important part of the new offensive plan would be entrusted to the ten panzer and four motorized infantry divisions. The vast majority of the German Army in the west, however, would still rely on horses for transportation.

They would be needed. Although the campaign in Poland had not been costly in terms of casualties, serious losses in vehicles had been suffered. The campaign had cost the army some

5,000 vehicles and 300 tanks.[28] Replacements for these were not forthcoming. This was what led General Franz Halder to consider the demotorization plan mentioned at the beginning of the chapter. Yet, substituting horses for vehicles also had its limits. Halder observed that if each infantry division used 4,500 horses and 2,000 horse-drawn vehicles, the army would have a shortage of horses by 1941.[29] Nevertheless, in spite of tremendous efforts, the army was still going to fall well short of the 16,000 trucks it required for the campaign.[30] The difference would have to be made up by horses.

But where were they to come from? To mobilize too many horses from Germany itself would simply be to repeat the mistake made by the army in World War I, for which German agriculture and food production paid.[31] The answer was ultimately supplied by Poland. The requisitioning of horses from Poland had been discontinued but was to begin again on 1 April 1940. Some 4,000 horses per week were to be delivered to the army from Poland.[32] In fact, the German command in Poland (OB East) estimated that Poland could yield as many as 100,000 horses in the period from 27 March to 14 May 1940.[33] All told, the German Army requisitioned some 148,000 horses from Germany and the occupied territories.[34]

Meanwhile, preparations for the invasion went forward. After the Polish campaign, most of the divisions were sent back to the west to get ready for the coming campaign. The unusually harsh winter presented units with additional problems for the horses in their care. For example, the 31st Infantry Division, which was stationed in Germany during the winter, reported that the horses suffered in the severe weather from chest ailments and colds in the respiratory tract.[35]

As the spring arrived, the Army's horses still suffered from health problems in some areas. The 231st Infantry Division, for example, was in Poland in the spring of 1940.[36] By mid-April the division was effectively paralyzed by an epidemic of equine pneumonia.[37]

Along the western front, the German Army assembled its forces and equipment, including horses. Army quartermasters

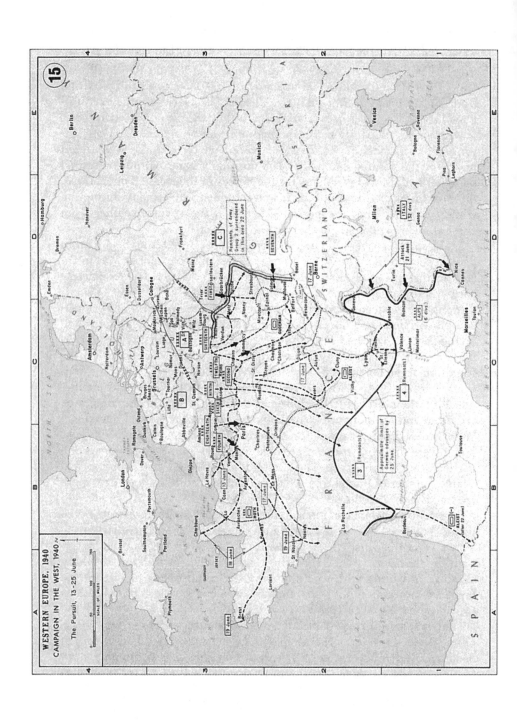

WESTERN EUROPE, 1940
CAMPAIGN IN THE WEST, 1940

The Pursuit, 13–25 June

kept a careful watch on the condition of the horses in their component divisions. The quartermaster of the Fourth Army, for example, filed a series of reports on the condition of the horses in its divisions. While most were good, some divisions were severely criticized for carelessness in the care and maintenance of their horses.[38] In such cases not only would the troops be criticized, but far more criticism would be directed at the regimental and battalion-level veterinarians for not providing proper supervision. Also noted were divisions that were employing large numbers of horses of a particularly delicate breed. The 32nd Infantry Division, for example, had a large number of Rhenish cold bloods, which required a good deal more special care and feeding.[39]

One curious instance of indiscipline on the part of the troops was noted by the jaundiced eye of the Fourth Army quartermaster. The quartermaster was upset because the troops of the most feared mechanized juggernaut in the world were throwing away bailing wire: the resulting shortage of bailing wire was hindering the compressing of hay for the horses.[40] In addition, all horse manure was to be collected and sent to Germany for use as fertilizer.[41]

The campaign proved to be a tremendous success for German arms, although the crossing of the Meuse River and the subsequent victory at Sedan proved much more of a near defeat than has commonly been thought.[42] The rigorous training program implemented after the Polish campaign yielded great results, as the quality of the conduct of the troops in combat showed marked improvement. The weather cooperated once again, as the spring of 1940 was unusually dry. Field Marshal Gerd von Rundstedt later noted that the extremely favorable weather enjoyed by the Germans in the Polish and French campaigns lured the German Army into a false sense of security with regard to the problems horses experience in bad weather.[43] In addition, the Luftwaffe quickly gained complete air superiority.

For the German Army's stock of horses, the campaign was a hard one, although experiences varied. One regiment reported that the condition of its horses actually improved during the campaign, as the weather was fine and fodder abundant.[44] Other experiences were different. The quartermaster of the 218th Infantry Division, for example, noted that the division's advance into the Vosges required constant moving by the divisional veterinary services, which made adequate care for the horses difficult to render.[45]

The pace of the advance was hard on the infantry divisions, who were constantly struggling to catch up with the far-ranging panzer divisions. Even the 218th Infantry Division, operating in a relatively minor sector in June, noted that the division's artillery draft horses were showing signs of exhaustion.[46] Of course, matters were much more difficult for the divisions operating in the areas of Army Groups A and B. To insure the smooth flow of traffic, army headquarters issued regulations concerning the establishment and maintenance of lines of communication.[47] Even these measures did not always attain the desired result. The 98th Infantry Division's units, marching in dispersed formation, stretched back along roads for thirty miles. The troops also discovered that a march of fifteen to twenty miles marked the limit of endurance for the horses.[48]

Casualties could be heavy at times. The 31st Infantry Division, operating in Belgium, lost 230 horses killed and 485 wounded in its initial commitment in combat.[49] The only way many units could maintain their required level of transportation was by the use of horses captured from the French Army or taken from the civilian population. The VIII Corps quartermaster allowed troops to use captured French Army horses as well as "ownerless" horses they picked up along the way, provided they were given medical and seriological examinations.[50] Troops would also exchange their own worn-out horses for fresh ones from peasants. These last two ways of obtaining remounts proved so tempting for the troops, however, that shortly after the onset of the final offensive in early June, OKH ordered troops to regard only horses belonging to the French Army as legitimate captures.[51]

Caring for the sick and wounded horses also made tremendous demands on the troops. The 218th Infantry Division had suffered some serious horse casualties from French artillery fire on the night of 15–16 June. Trucks had to be used to get replacements to the front, and wounded horses had to be evacuated to hospitals. All this was done by truck. The division veterinarian, Colonel Doctor Lueger, highly commended the truck drivers, as accomplishing these tasks called for them to drive continuously for as long as thirty hours.[52]

Generally, however, casualties were relatively light. By 17 June 1940, Army Group A had suffered 90,000 horse casualties, Army Group B 24, and Army Group C 337.[53] These figures evidently included horses that were only sick, as that was the primary cause of casualties among horses.

The Germans derived great strategic benefits from the conquest of France and the Low Countries. The Breton ports were to play an important part in Admiral Karl Dönitz's U-boat effort in the battle of the Atlantic. The vast economic resources of the west also made an important contribution to the Germany war economy. By 1941, of the 32.5 million tons of steel produced by Germany and the occupied territories, some 11.7 million tons (36 percent) came out of the occupied areas.[54] Germany's fuel situation improved in two important ways: First, with the campaign in the west virtually decided, Hitler sought to strengthen Germany's ties to Romanian oil sources. To that end, on 27 May 1940 Germany signed the "Oil Pact" with Romania, by which Germany would trade arms for oil.[55] In addition, although France did not produce a great deal of oil, all of France's oil installations were captured intact when attempts to demolish them were botched.[56] Large numbers of vehicles were captured, so that it was indeed true that the invasion of the Soviet Union could not have been undertaken without the multitude of captured French vehicles.[57]

The German Army also gained horses. Control of France and the Low Countries now gave Germany access to the horse-breeding areas of Holland and Normandy. In addition, the

Germans had captured the French Army's stock of horses. Toward the end of the campaign and in its immediate aftermath, the rounding up of captured horses became one of the primary tasks of the infantry divisions. During the period 22 to 30 June 1940 alone the 218th Infantry Division collected some 9,000 captured horses.[58] Captured horses were convoyed to army veterinary examining stations by French prisoners, one man for every three horses. The German Army would provide the guards, blacksmiths, and veterinary staff.[59] The horses were examined for any symptoms of contagious disease. Once examined and pronounced fit, they would then be sent either to army horse parks or back to Germany.[60] In fact, by 1 August 1940, some 34,000 horses had been sent back to Germany from Holland, Belgium, and occupied France.[61]

With the successful conclusion of the battle of France, the Germans confronted the problem of invading England. Although the Luftwaffe's failure over Britain rendered the question moot, it is unlikely that a successful invasion could have been mounted for several reasons: First, the Norwegian campaign, as noted previously, had effectively destroyed the small German surface navy. This reduced Germany's amphibious capacity, never formidable to begin with, to an extremely low level. Also, even in an amphibious invasion, the German Army could not do without horses. As formulated Operation Sea Lion called for the transportation of 170,000 men, 57,500 horses, and 34,000 vehicles from the French coast to England in several waves.[62] The invasion forces would be carried to England in a rather motley collection of merchant ships, barges, tugs, motor boats, and yachts.[63] The plan even called for 4,200 horses to accompany the first wave and for 7,000 more to accompany the second, figures that caused Halder rather grave misgivings.[64] One indeed shudders at the image of teams of horses being driven on to a defended beach. Finally, Admiral Eberhart Weichold of the Naval High Command (OKM) believed that even if the Luftwaffe had been able to defeat Fighter Command over southern England,

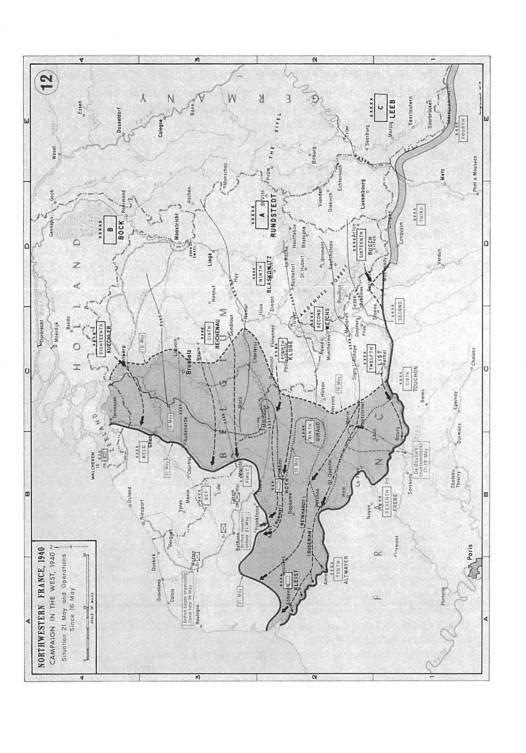

NORTHWESTERN FRANCE, 1940
CAMPAIGN IN THE WEST, 1940
Situation 21 May and Operations
Since 16 May

SCALE OF MILES

Hitler, with his instinctive dislike of amphibious operations, still would have hesitated to launch Sea Lion.[65]

In any case, it did not matter. The Luftwaffe's failure against Fighter Command insured that there would be no invasion in any case. Instead, Hitler turned his gaze towards the east.

CHAPTER 3

Barbarossa

[On the advance] a very large number of horses had died. Many were lagging behind, wasting away, wandering at the rear; others followed their corps, to whom they were a useless embarrassment.

Armand de Caulaincourt[1]

When *Barbarossa* begins, the world will hold its breath.

Adolf Hitler[2]

During the interval between the fall of France and the invasion of the Soviet Union, the German Army became involved in two other campaigns, of which one will receive no more than passing mention in our study. In January 1941 Hitler sent a small motorized force, the *Deutsches Afrika Korps*, under the soon to be renowned General Erwin Rommel, to Tripoli to bolster the Italian position in North Africa. Although the North African campaign lasted until the Axis surrender on 13 May 1943, it will not concern us directly as none of the combatants—Germany, Italy, and the Commonwealth powers—used horses in the desert, for obvious reasons.

In the spring of 1941, again to bolster the Italians, Germany invaded Yugoslavia and Greece. To undertake the operation, the Twelfth Army and the First Panzer Group had eight infantry, three mountain, two panzer, and two motorized infantry divisions—380,000 men and 65,000 horses altogether.[3] Units employing horses and mules were important in the campaign because of the mountainous terrain over which it was conducted, although it should also be pointed out that panzer divisions such as the 11th spent the winter of 1940/41 training for

THE BALKANS, 1941
INVASION OF YUGOSLAVIA
AND GREECE, APRIL 1941

NOTES

1. Yugoslavian field army locations shown represent planned dispositions for defense— in a cordon arrangement. When the German attack came, the Yugoslavs were still mobilizing; only the regular divisions of the Third and Fifth Armies were fully mobilized.

There were some Frontier Guard battalions in position, but, in general, Yugoslav defenses were disorganized, and units were committed piecemeal.

2. Elements of W Force began arriving in Greece on 7 March. The force ultimately totaled about 30,000 and was comprised of the British 1st Armored Brigade, the 6th Australian Division, the 2d New Zealand Division, and supporting troops.

3. Cut off as a result of the advance of elements of the XL Panzer Corps, the Greek First Army surrendered on 20 April. The Second Army had capitulated earlier, on 9 April.

4. Kleist's First Panzer Group originally was designated for employment in the invasion of Greece, under Twelfth Army. With the decision to invade Yugoslavia, it's mission was changed to participate in that operation, although the XI Corps was never utilized in either invasion. About 10 April, however, the 5th Panzer Division was transferred to the Twelfth Army control (to XL Panzer Corps).

5. Note that the preliminaries to the successful penetration of Central Greece were really part of the Yugoslavian invasion—the isolation of Yugoslavia from British-Greek help (advance of the 9th and 2nd Panzer Divisions, commencing on 6 April).

17

operations in mountainous terrain, which paid fine dividends in the campaign.[4]

For the purposes of this book, the Balkan campaign has several points of interest: First, the German Army was seriously short of fuel at the height of its power. On 28 November 1940 OKH reported to OKW that the newly established monthly allocations of gasoline and diesel fuel were wholly inadequate for even relatively minor operations, including the projected Balkan campaign.[5]

Second, this was the first time infantry divisions were subordinated directly to a panzer group headquarters. This created problems when the divisions attached to General Ewald von Kleist's First Panzer Group moved into Bulgaria before the beginning of the operation. Since no army-level veterinary services were available for those divisions, the divisional veterinary company was responsible for everything. If horses became too ill to move, the only thing the veterinary companies could do was to report their location to the veterinary officer of the German Army Mission in Romania. Unit commanders were authorized to make purchases but were forbidden to make requisitions in any case.[6]

Finally, the subordination of infantry divisions to the First Panzer Group continued through the campaign. The quartermaster of the First Panzer Group noted after the campaign in Yugoslavia that combining infantry and mobile divisions did not work well logistically. The task of supplying infantry divisions should have been left to the army headquarters.[7]

Losses in the campaign were rather light. Total losses in the Twelfth Army for the month of April amounted to about twelve thousand, of which only about five thousand were actual combat casualties.[8] Losses in combat vehicles for the First Panzer Group were extremely small—only 3 percent in the Yugoslavian campaign. Losses in cars and trucks were compensated by the fact that most captured Yugoslavian vehicles were of German origin.[9] All the while, the Wehrmacht was preparing for its greatest undertaking.

Hitler planned to invade the Soviet Union in 1941 with as large a motorized force as possible. To this end, the number of panzer divisions was doubled, according to the OKH order of 26 September 1940.[10] Yet, the increasing of the number of panzer divisions to an apparently impressive total of twenty-one, and of motorized infantry divisions to fourteen (of which four were SS), betrayed the German Army's lack of modernity. A large number of vehicles were of French manufacture, and a large number of tanks were made in Czechoslovakia. This large influx of foreign material, plus the German propensity to build a number of different versions of the same vehicle, meant that the German Army would invade the Soviet Union with over two thousand different types of vehicles, which would make field maintenance a nightmare.[11]

Germany's oil situation was equally precarious. Germany had increased its oil imports from Romania to 2,114,000 tons by 1941.[12] This was to prove completely inadequate to meet the requirements for the 1941 campaign. Thus, even the most modern elements of the German Army were poorly equipped for the invasion.

Despite efforts to increase the level of motorization of the German Army, the vast majority of the German Army's divisions would be marching infantry. Of the 145 divisions committed to Operation Barbarossa, some 113 were infantry, a sizeable increase over the force that had invaded France and the Low Countries the year before. This, of course, required an immense increase in the number of horses in the German Army. One of the main sources for horses was to be Poland, as noted in the previous chapter. Additionally, Poland was to provide some fifteen thousand peasant carts to give the infantry divisions additional transportation.[13] These carts were to be allocated by the *General Gouvernement*, with about two hundred carts going to each division.[14]

Other preparations also had to be taken. During World War I, German units operating in Russia had a very difficult time coping with the dreaded disease of glanders.[15] The veterinary office of OKH issued guidelines and regulations for observing preventative measures against the disease, and these proved quite successful. Additionally, there were those ailments peculiar to Russia, in particular primoplasmosis and anaplasmosis. The veterinary office issued a manual for the treatment of these diseases to all units.[16] The period before the invasion was not exactly free of medical problems, however. During the autumn of 1940, the Fourth Army reported serious losses due to a cholic epidemic.[17]

Meanwhile, the collection of horses went on. Immediately after the conclusion of the French campaign, the equine resources of France were organized. Troops in the Fourth Army were given instructions regarding French stud farms similar to those received by the Tenth Army in Poland.[18] All captured horses were to be given sereological and bacteriological examinations. French civilian veterinarians from the Pasteur Institute of Paris were employed to assist in administering the examinations.[19]

After the French campaign, the process of weeding out unfit horses and incorporating replacements was also initiated. Local commanders in France had the latitude to sell horses unfit for military service to farmers. Horses unfit for either military service or agriculture could be sold to the civilian population for slaughter. Once accepted, captured horses were to be branded with a distinctive "H" on the left flank.[20]

Local commanders could purchase horses from the farmers to whom they sold their worn-out horses. In both cases, the sale and purchase prices were set by the army.[21] Although no numbers seem to be available, one can rest assured that the Wehrmacht's purchase and sale prices for horses were set to give maximum financial advantage to the Germans.

The situation in Poland was somewhat different from that in France, as just described. The Fourth Army—the largest of the armies in Army Group Center—while assembling in the autumn and winter of 1940/41, was strictly prohibited from requisitioning or drafting horses in the area of the *General Gouvernement*. Horses were to be obtained through standard army procedures.[22]

Theoretically, it was to be that way in the Soviet Union as well. According to German occupation policy postulated before the invasion, the invading armies were to be fed by Soviet agriculture.[23] As Soviet agriculture was still based mainly on horses for tractive power, the obtaining of horses would have to be handled with care, as the drafting of too many would disrupt the agriculture. OKH made sure to impress this on the troops.[24] The situation was made more delicate by the parlous state of the Soviet Union's horse population, on which forced collectivization and the ensuing terror-famine had inflicted grievous losses. From 1928 to 1933, the Soviet Union's horse population declined from 32 million to 17 million, a 47 percent decrease.[25] These losses had not nearly been made good, and thus care would be needed in drafting indigenous Soviet horses. All captured Soviet Army horses were to be sent to German Army veterinary services for examination. Captured Soviet Army veterinary officers and blacksmiths were to be employed in caring for the captured horses.[26]

The German Army that was to invade the Soviet Union consisted of eighteen panzer, thirteen motorized infantry, and seventy-eight infantry divisions. There were also eight mountain and light infantry divisions, as well as several security divisions.[27] The disparity in the marching capabilities between the mobile and infantry formations played an important part in the planning of the invasion, because the Soviet Union presented an added complexity avoided in the earlier campaigns—space. Those planning the invasion had divided into two factions: Hitler and OKW preferred a plan emphasizing the capture of the Soviet Union's economically valuable areas, while Halder and OKH wanted to concentrate on the immediate defeat of the Soviet armies along the border.[28] The ultimate result was a compromise plan that called for a general advance through the Baltic states in the north, the Ukraine in the south, and up to Smolensk in the area of Army Group Center. Only after that would the final objectives be decided.[29]

Yet, even the plan accepted by both Hitler and Halder produced disagreements among the commanders chosen to execute it. Although all were agreed that the Soviet armies should be destroyed as close as possible to the frontier, there was disagreement as to how deep the encirclement should be. Guderian gave the impression in *Panzer Leader* that his initial objective was Smolensk.[30] The plan as developed by the headquarters staff, however, called for the armored pincers to close at Minsk, some 150 miles west of Smolensk.[31] The shorter encirclements were preferred because it was feared that with longer-range envelopments the infantry divisions could not catch up with the far-ranging panzers. The rings of encirclement would thus be too loose, and many Soviets could escape.

There were also disagreements in the tactical planning. Who should make the initial assault to effect the breakthrough? The field army commanders wanted the infantry to make the initial assault, through which the panzer groups would rush to initiate the exploitation. Guderian wanted his formations to make the initial assault and then drive deep into the Soviet rear.[32] He was supported in this by his fellow panzer group commander, General Hermann Hoth.[33] The panzer generals feared that if the panzer divisions were deployed behind the infantry divisions, they would be slowed down considerably by the horse-drawn columns of the infantry formations, which would clog up the few available roads. Ultimately, the panzer commanders got their way, although in cases where tanks were unsuitable, such as taking the fortress of Brest-Litovsk, the infantry would go in first.

The completion of the preparations for Barbarossa represented a tremendous logistical achievement for the German Army, although the invasion was launched on a logistical shoestring when compared to later American standards. By mid-June the Germans had amassed some 3 million men, 600,000 vehicles, 3,350 tanks, and 2,000 aircraft along the border.[34] The number of horses given tends to vary rather widely with sources. A standard American source gives the number of horses as being 625,000.[35] A 1967 German work gives the lowest figure, only 600,000.[36] A more recent German work sets the number as high as 750,000.[37]

Since the major effort was to be made by Army Group Center, this army group was given the largest force, consisting of the Fourth and Ninth Armies, plus the Second and Third Panzer Groups, under the overall command of Field Marshal Fedor von Bock. This command also contained the most tanks and had the most aircraft in support. If we accept the higher total figure for horses, the horses were divided relatively evenly among the army groups, each of which had two armies. Perhaps the largest single army, horsewise, was Field Marshal Gunther von Kluge's Fourth Army, which by 13 June 1941 contained 130,000 horses, of which some 125,970 were in Poland.[38] Bock's other army, Colonel General Adolf Strauss's Ninth Army, had 87,000 horses.[39]

The opening stages of the invasion provided the Wehrmacht with a combination of stunning victories and subtle failures. Field Marshal Wilhelm von Leeb's Army Group North quickly cleared the Baltic states, but failed to envelop the Soviet 8th and 11th Armies. The advance then became temporarily stalled at the Dvina River. Rundstedt's Army Group South encountered the toughest initial resistance, but Kleist's First Panzer Group eventually broke through and encircled a large Soviet force at the battle of Uman, yielding a bag of 103,000 prisoners.[40] Nevertheless, Army Group South's major objective, the Ukrainian capital of Kiev, still remained in Soviet hands by the end of August. Army Group Center scored stunning successes. One week after the start of the invasion Guderian's and Hoth's panzer groups met at Minsk. The Bialystock and Minsk pockets yielded some 290,000 prisoners. With Minsk secure, Hoth and Guderian repeated the same maneuver at Smolensk, again trapping a large bag of prisoners.

After Smolensk's fall on 16 July, Hitler vacillated over his next move. His generals, especially those in Army Group Center, wanted to make the next thrust at Moscow. Hitler, however, wanted to secure Leningrad in the north and the vast economic resources of the Ukraine in the south. Ultimately, he halted Army Group Center's advance and sent Hoth's Third Panzer Group north to Leningrad, while Guderian's Second Panzer Group was sent south into the Ukraine.

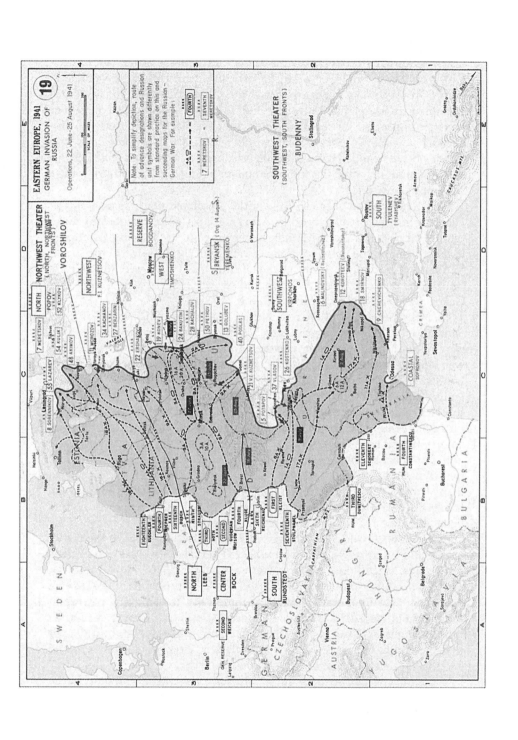

EASTERN EUROPE, 1941

19

GERMAN INVASION OF
RUSSIA

Operations, 22 June–25 August 1941

SCALE OF MILES

Note: To simplify depiction, route
of advance designations and Russian
unit symbols are shown differently
from standard practice on this and
succeeding maps for the Russian–
German War. For example:

7 MERETSKOV = SEVENTH
MERETSKOV

NORTHWEST THEATER
(NORTH, NORTHWEST
FRONTS)

VOROSHILOV

SOUTHWEST THEATER
(SOUTHWEST, SOUTH FRONTS)

BUDENNY

The Ukrainian operation resulted in the battle of Kiev, yielding an enormous bag of 665,000 prisoners, but at the cost of four to six weeks of rapidly dwindling favorable weather. In the north, Army Group North was able to breach the Dvina line, but was eventually stopped short of Leningrad by the combination of tough Soviet resistance, bad weather, and shifting German priorities. It was not until the end of September that the Wehrmacht was ready to make its final thrust toward Moscow.

Although the 1941 invasion had produced great victories, as the campaign wore on it also exposed the flaws inherent in the German Army. As noted previously, the German Army entered the Soviet Union with over two thousand different types of vehicles. But even with the use of so many captured foreign vehicles, the German Army was short some 2,700 trucks at the start of the campaign.[41] As the campaign wore on matters became worse for several reasons. One of these was that many of the captured French vehicles were not well suited to conditions in the Soviet Union and broke down. German wheeled vehicles also had tremendous difficulties, since many of them were actually civilian vehicles and not suited to military operations.[42] To add to these problems, the German economy was still operating at a peacetime pace, thus making it difficult to make good on losses. As a result, truck losses began to outrun production in August.[43] Thus, as the German Army drove deeper and deeper into the Soviet Union, it became steadily less motorized. Horses would eventually have to make up the difference.

While the German Army's motor vehicles were having problems in the Soviet Union, the summer campaign also had not been exactly kind to the German Army's horses. The first obvious problem was climate. Climatically, the Soviet Union is a land of extremes. The severity of the Russian winter is well known. Less renowned is the severity of the Russian summer, which, though short, can be extremely hot. This had a terrible effect on the horses, who had to march long distances to keep up with the advance. Long and frequent halts had to be taken to water the horses.[44]

Feed was also a problem. As stated previously, oats was considered by the German Army to be the best feed for horses. Oats, however, were not widely sown in the Soviet Union. Although green fodder was available in abundance, it could only be utilized under certain circumstances. For example, the 21st Infantry Division, part of Army Group North, was able to make extensive use of green fodder during July.[45] This was because Army Group North spent much of July held up on the line of the Dvina. The 12th Infantry Division—also part of Army Group North—operating in the Kholm area during much of August, collected some 760 tons of hay from 24 July to 31 August.[46] The divisions of Army Group Center were also able to make use of green fodder, as the army group's active operations halted with the moves to the flanks and the evacuation of the Yelnya salient. In Army Group South, the fairly constant tempo of operations made the collection of green or raw fodder extremely difficult.[47]

One area where the Germans were spared difficulty was disease. Although mange was relatively common, it was easily treated with sulphur dioxide introduced in a special type of gas chamber possessed by every horse hospital. The preventative measures taken by the German Army against glanders were completely successful. Although many Soviet farm animals showed symptoms of glanders, at no time did the German Army ever experience problems with this disease, as they had in World War I.[48] The same was true of the disease piroplasmosis, which, by the twentieth century, was rare in the West.[49]

The German Army's reliance on horses in this campaign also presented a number of problems strategically, tactically, and logistically that had not been encountered in previous campaigns. Strategically, the drastic dichotomy in the marching capabilities between the panzer and motorized infantry divisions and the nonmotorized infantry divisions led to problems almost immediately. In Army Group Center, although the panzer commanders had had their way on the initial deployment of their divisions, problems still cropped up. As the panzer groups moved quickly forward, they found themselves running into supply problems, as their supply columns were blocked by the infantry divisions still crossing the bridges over the Bug River.[50] In addition, as the panzer groups moved ever forward, they became ever more separated from the infantry divisions. Even though the infantry divisions were setting march records on an almost daily basis, they never could catch up. Thus, even though the armored pincers were able to meet first at Minsk on 27 June and again at Smolensk on 16 July, the net could not be drawn tightly enough because of the gap between the mobile formations and the infantry units. Thus, although Army Group Center was able to secure two large bags of prisoners, many Soviet soldiers were able to escape through the loosely drawn net.[51]

Tactically, the Germans were having problems with horses. Throughout the campaign German units found that their horse-drawn columns were vulnerable to air attack. As early as 24 June, the 1st Cavalry Division, part of Army Group Center, was subjected to two Soviet bombing attacks that inflicted heavy losses in horses.[52] In Army Group North, the 21st Infantry Division veterinarian reported serious horse losses from air attack on 25 June.[53] The 23rd Infantry Division had similar complaints on 4 August.[54] These losses were incurred during a period in the campaign of complete German air superiority. This vulnerability to even such limited attack did not augur well for the future.

Another tactical problem experienced by German veterinary units was sudden encounters with retreating or cut-off Soviet troops. On 27 June the Horse Collection Station of the 44th Infantry Division was attacked in Lokacze by Soviet soldiers who had been bypassed in the German advance. In the resulting encounter, three Soviet soldiers were killed.[55] The 21st Infantry Division's veterinary company had encountered so many Soviet soldiers at various times in its advance that the veterinary officer of the division requested the allocation of two extra-light machine guns and additional rifles for the company.[56]

Logistical problems began to crop up early on, largely due to the failure of the Germans to solve the problem of converting the broad-gauge Soviet rail track to the narrower European gauge. Railway construction companies were far too few for the task at hand. In addition, the allocation of construction companies could not begin until after the offensive had made sufficient progress to allow the condition of the various lines to be assessed. Construction companies were also limited in their efforts because they lacked motor transport, relying instead on construction trains.[57] All this meant that, despite the best efforts of the construction companies, the development of the rail system proceeded slowly. By 10 July, although some three hundred miles of track had been converted, the capacity of the lines was still too low to be of major help.[58]

Valuable rail transport space had to be devoted to fuel and ammunition. The standard European freight car could carry at most only eight light draft horses. Heavier draft horses required more space, so that a car could carry either six heavy draft horses or only four extra-heavy draft horses.[59] Given the relative scarcity of rail transportation space, replacement horses had to be marched to the front.[60] While not an immediate problem, it rapidly assumed nightmarish dimensions. From 22 June to 10 July, Army Group North had advanced some 180 miles, Army Group South 120 miles, and Army Group Center an astonishing 285 miles.[61] Marching replacement horses to the front over such distances could often wear them out before they could even be put to work at the front.

Equipment also became hard to replace; in fact, the German Army even ran short of feed bags. The feed bags, which were made of cotton, wore out after several months of constant use. The Germans were able to improvise a portable wooden trough, which could be used to feed up to three horses simultaneously, but this created conditions that promoted the spread of contagious disease.[62]

Horse losses, replacements, and remounts also began to provide difficulties. Losses began to mount early in the campaign. The most severely affected horses were the heavy and extra-heavy draft horses, which were used mainly for hauling artillery.[63] These units tended to suffer most from air attack.

Also, heavy warm bloods and extra-heavy cold bloods were rather delicate creatures. They were more susceptible to extremes of temperature and required more fodder and water, demands that could not always be met during the advance.

To make matters worse, there were not enough of these animals, or army horses in general, available as replacements. For the 44th Infantry Division, operating in the Ukraine, losses had begun to outrun replacements fairly quickly. By 31 July, the division had lost about 7 percent of its horses, even with replacements.[64] At the other end of the front, the 21st Infantry Division noted on 7 August 1941 that lighter horses would have to be used in tasks normally performed by heavy draft horses because replacements simply were not available.[65]

Obtaining replacements in itself was often difficult. German divisions generally went into the campaign with a reserve of only 150 horses, at best.[66] The 30th Infantry Division's veterinarian reported that the division went into the campaign with a mere forty-five horses available in the veterinary company's reserve section.[67] These small numbers were exhausted quickly, and replacements, as stated previously, had to be driven forward overland across great distances. The alternatives were to obtain horses either from the Soviet Army or from the local civilian population.

Like the German Army, the Soviet Army of 1941 was largely dependent on horses for transport. The standard 1941 Soviet Army rifle division contained about 14,500 men.[68] Estimating from its organizational structure, the division employed between thirty-five hundred and four thousand horses.[69] The quality of the Soviet Army's horses was generally good, but they were not captured in large numbers. The 21st Infantry Division in Army Group North, for example, reported the capture of only small numbers of Soviet Army horses.[70] The 260th Infantry Division, operating under Army Group Center, from 19 July to 11 September 1941 captured only 327 horses, certainly not enough to keep pace with the losses suffered.[71] In seeking to understand why the German Army captured so few Soviet Army horses, it must be borne in mind that the Soviets were operating under conditions very similar to those experienced by the Germans in Normandy in 1944. With German aircraft rampaging all along the front, Soviet transport columns drawn by horses made easy marks for the Luftwaffe.

Horses were obtained locally in the Soviet Union, as the Germans were to occupy a total area that had a horse population of 11 million.[72] The quality of these horses, however, varied considerably. The 21st Infantry Division, operating in Lithuania, found that Lithuanian horses were of such poor quality as to be completely useless.[73] The most common horses found in the Soviet Union proper were the panje horses, small animals of great toughness. These were quickly pressed into service. The Germans quickly found, however, that this created a new problem, this time with equipment. The standard German artillery piece, a 105mm howitzer, when loaded with fodder, ammunition, and equipment—the gun and limber were driven as a single unit weighed as much as four tons—a difficult task even for six well-fed heavy draft horses.[74] The heavy artillery gun, a 150mm piece, with gun and limber driven separately, required eight horses just to haul the reserve cart, which carried the ammunition.[75] Panje horses were far too small and light for hauling artillery. They were also unsuited to hauling horse-drawn vehicles. The standard German Army horse-drawn vehicle was made of steel, which also proved too heavy for the small panje horses.[76] Here, however, the two hundred Polish carts allocated to each infantry division before the invasion proved to be invaluable. Wooden vehicles were also obtained locally.[77]

After the conclusion of operations in the Kiev area, the German Army prepared for what Hitler and the OKH High Command believed would be the final offensive and conclusion of the campaign. The major thrust would be undertaken by Army Group Center, which now consisted of the Second Panzer Group, temporarily named *Armeegruppe Guderian*, as well as the Third and Fourth Panzer Groups, along with the Second, Fourth, and Ninth Armies.[78] The offensive would have to be launched quickly, as the good campaigning weather was rapidly running out.

The offensive, launched on 30 September, got off to a brilliant start. Army Group Center once again employed its patented encircling maneuver, which resulted in the twin encirclements at Vyazma and Bryansk, yielding another 665,000 prisoners. This success was due to two reasons: First, the Germans achieved complete surprise. The Soviet High Command (STAVKA) was not expecting a major German offensive so late in the campaigning season, and thus was clearly caught off guard.[79] Also, unlike previous encirclement operations, this time the panzers closed the rings after a relatively short thrust, allowing the infantry divisions moving up to draw the net tight fairly quickly.

Although the offensive had gotten off to a successful start, problems appeared immediately. Theoretically, the horse situation for the infantry divisions should have been good, as no major offensive operations had been undertaken by Army Group Center between the end of July and the end of September. While the operations at Kiev and Leningrad were taking place, however, the Soviets conducted a series of attacks against Army Group Center's positions. While not strategically threatening in any way, the Soviet attacks did cause casualties, especially to the horses in the infantry and to artillery elements in the infantry divisions.[80] The mobile divisions also were in a parlous state. They had been conducting operations almost continuously since 22 June, and many of their vehicles were in poor condition. The XXIV Panzer Corps, for example, had not been able to perform one day of maintenance on its vehicles after 22 June 1941.[81]

An equally serious problem was the weather. Although the weather at the start of the operation was quite good, it deteriorated rapidly. It turned colder and precipitation followed. Guderian noted that the first snowfall, on the night of 6–7 October, melted and transformed the dirt roads into bottomless canals of mud.[82] This quickly slowed the German advance to a crawl. Only tracked vehicles could make any headway.

Trucks and other wheeled vehicles sank up to their axles. The First Panzer Army, logistically hamstrung by mud and vehicle losses, began hiring peasants with their horses and vehicles for temporary service. A teamster with one horse and wagon was paid at a per diem rate of fifty rubles. A teamster with two horses and a wagon could earn seventy rubles a day. The peasants had to provide fodder for their own horses along the line of march.[83] The horses themselves struggled forward over heavy ground in the worsening weather, something the Germans had not had to deal with in their earlier campaigns.[84] Consequently, exhaustion now became a problem for the German Army's horses. In the 30th Infantry Division between 16 September and 30 November 1941, for example, the division's veterinary company and horse collection stations dealt with a total of 1,072 horses. Of this total, only 117 were wounded. The rest were suffering from exhaustion.[85]

With the weather deteriorating rapidly and a large pocket to mop up, the Germans probably should have halted all operations right then, but Hitler and OKH decided that the offensive was to resume once the ground had hardened with frost, which would not be until November. By that time, panzer divisions averaged only about one-third of their normal strength. Infantry divisions had only 65 percent of their horse-drawn transportation available.[86] Horse losses had also mounted alarmingly, totaling 102,910 killed and 33,314 sick or rendered otherwise unfit for service.[87]

The offensive resumed on 15 November 1941. It made some quick gains, and by early December some patrols reached a point from which the spires of the Kremlin could be observed. This, however, was the high water mark of the German effort. The Soviets, commanded by the able Marshal Georgi Zhukov, launched a well-timed counterattack that pushed Army Group Center back, and that was later developed into a general strategic offensive by Joseph Stalin and STAVKA. The German lines, especially in the area of Army Group Center, were driven back, with some Soviet penetrations reaching a depth of two hundred miles before the entire front stabilized at the end of February.[88]

The final German effort against Moscow, and the ensuing Soviet counteroffensive, produced a grave crisis in the German Army. Large numbers of vehicles, many of French design, either broke down or were unsuitable for winter operations.[89] Total German truck losses for November alone were 5,996, slightly more than double the production of 2,752 for the same month.[90] The difference had to be made up by horses, even in the panzer divisions, such as the 5th, which used horses and sleds for transportation in the winter.[91] In fact, horse-drawn columns were considered to be the only certain means of supply in the winter.[92]

The sufferings of the lightly clad German soldiers in the harsh Russian winter are well documented. Yet, the situation for horses was just as bad. The heavy Western European breeds especially suffered severely. Army Group Center's horse losses reached about one thousand per day during the winter.[93] Many more horses were rendered weak or unfit by exposure. This severely affected the artillery of the infantry divisions. The 7th Infantry Division reported that ten horses were required to haul a light field piece. A heavy field gun (150mm) could also be drawn by ten horses, but only on well-paved roads.[94] The XX Corps reported that while four horses could draw a light artillery piece, as many as ten to sixteen were needed for heavy artillery.[95]

Sleds were used for supplies and other equipment, but here again German equipment was too heavy. All the after-action reports at every level agree that German Army sleds were too heavy for the small Russian panje horses, as well as for German Army horses grown gaunt and weak from extended campaigning.[96] Russian sleds were considered better, with the light panje sled drawn by a single panje horse being the best.[97]

Aside from the Soviet Army, the German Army's stock of horses had to cope with the problems of weather, disease, and lack of fodder. Although moving German units were instructed to stop for rest only near villages where the horses could be given shelter, finding such locations was no easy task in the devastated Soviet countryside.[98]

Disease was also a problem. Although spared epidemics of serious diseases such as glanders, mange became a serious problem. The quartermaster of the Fourth Army reported that by 8 December 1941, ten divisions had reported serious outbreaks of mange.[99] This problem was aggravated by the weather, as the winter of 1941–42 in the Soviet Union was the worst in over a century.[100] Normally, mange is a disease easily treatable, but to operate effectively, operation chambers had to be located in an easily heatable area, a requirement not easily met in the frigid Russian winter.[101] Because of the need for horses, slightly infected horses were kept at the front, even though this increased the risk of contagion to uninfected horses.[102] Aside from mange, units also had to contend with pneumonia and frostbite cases in large numbers, with both men and horses affected.[103]

Under these circumstances, it is not surprising that German horse hospitals were overwhelmed by sheer numbers. Hospitals equipped to handle 500 to 550 horses now had to cope with 2,000 to 3,000 horses at a time.[104] Here, the Germans benefited from maintaining three horse hospitals per army. The Seventh Army noted the need for three hospitals to maintain an army with 130,000 horses, which had suffered an assured loss rate of only 5 percent before the French campaign.[105] Since even the mobile divisions had to employ horses, the panzer groups, now designated panzer armies, were assigned horse hospitals. The First Panzer Army, for example, did not even have a veterinary officer on its staff at the beginning of the campaign.[106] By 11 December 1941, however, the army had a strength of 400,000 men, 60,000 horses, and 45,000 vehicles. The horses were serviced by one horse hospital, one veterinary park, and two horse transport columns.[107] These measures were still insufficient, even though by October 1941 the German Army had some 24,000 veterinary troops in the Soviet Union.[108]

Fodder was also a difficult problem. Standard German Army fodder consisted of a cake composed mostly of oats and mixed with varying amounts of yeast, potato flakes, hay, and straw.[109] There was little in the way of oats available in the Soviet Union, however. Hard fodder had to be shipped to units by rail. This put an added burden on the already over-strained rail system. The problem was one of space: a ton of gasoline takes up only five cubic feet of space, while a ton of compressed fodder occupies five hundred cubic feet.[110] This was one of the reasons why the British theorist J.F.C. Fuller had advocated mechanization in the 1920s and 1930s.[111]

German units improvised as best they could under the circumstances. In the area of Army Group South barley was available and occasionally mixed with some oats.[112] More often than not, the most common materials used as fodder included straw, hay, linseed, and, at times, tree bark.[113] Horses had to be put on short rations, and this affected their ability to haul artillery.[114]

Yet, despite all these difficulties, the Wehrmacht survived. Ambulatory horses were evacuated, while those unfit for service and unable to be moved were slaughtered for meat. Some divisions decided to risk the loss of tactical mobility in order to save their horses. The 255th Infantry Division, for example, sent some eight hundred horses to Yartsevo, almost one hundred miles to the rear, to get horses feed and shelter.[115] Replacements were either brought up from the rear or obtained locally. Horse losses, however, had been unprecedentedly heavy. From 22 June 1941 to 20 March 1942, the German Army in the Soviet Union had lost some 264,954 horses killed, sick, or otherwise unfit for service.[116]

The German invasion of the Soviet Union failed in part because of the German Army's heavy reliance on the horse for transport. The Soviet spaces proved too vast to be overcome by what van Creveld has described as a "semi-motorized army."[117] The failure of the infantry divisions to draw the encircling nets tightly allowed significant numbers of Soviet troops to escape. The failure to completely destroy the Soviet armies at the outset of the campaign led the German Army, handicapped by inadequate logistical resources, uncertain strategy, and a vicious ideology, into an extended campaign for which it was not prepared.

Yet there is another side to this. While horses were in part responsible for the failure of the campaign, they were also the means of deliverance for the German Army during the winter crisis. Vehicle losses had been enormous. Of the 500,000 wheeled motor vehicles with which the Germans began the campaign, by mid-November 1941 only 75,000 (15 percent) were in good working order. Although the Germans had captured some 80,000 Russian vehicles, only 40 percent of those were in operating condition, and replacing them was impossible.[118] Without horse-drawn supply columns to keep the troops supplied in the winter, an even worse disaster would have befallen the German Army. The Wehrmacht had just survived its greatest trial thus far, but Stalingrad still lay ahead.

CHAPTER 4

From Near Victory to Certain Defeat: The German Army in the Soviet Union, 1942–1943

It must not happen that, by advancing too quickly and too far, armored and motorized formations lose connection with the infantry following them; or that they lose the opportunity of supporting the hard-pressed, forward-fighting infantry by direct attacks on the rear of the encircled Russian armies.

Adolf Hitler, 5 April 1942[1]

Preservation of the 7,300 troop horses is therefore considered highly desirable, in order that at least a portion of the heavy weapons and the divisional artillery should remain mobile. This would necessitate supply by air of 22 tons (3 kilos per horse) of fodder per day.

Army Group Don to OKH, 23 December 1942[2]

The last horses have been eaten up.

Friedrich von Paulus, 19 January 1943[3]

Whenever I think of this attack [Kursk] my stomach turns over.

Adolf Hitler, 10 May 1943[4]

In the 1941 campaign, the German Army came close to victory over the Soviet Union but was ultimately frustrated at Moscow. At least one authority has argued, correctly in my opinion, that by January 1942 a German victory over the Allied powers was no longer possible.[5] Even though the trials of 1941 had inflicted damage on the Wehrmacht, it was still a formidable fighting force by anyone's estimate. Hitler and OKH, however, were divided over the next course of action. The arduous campaign of 1941 had left the German Army deep inside the Soviet Union but too weak to resume the offensive all along the front. The best they could hope to do was to mass sufficient forces in one area for an offensive.

On this matter Hitler and Halder were divided. Halder wanted to wait a year, spending 1942 building up the army, and then resume the offensive along the entire front.[6] Hitler, however, would have none of that. He preferred an offensive by Army Group South. General Friedrich von Paulus's Sixth Army and Hoth's Fourth Panzer Army would drive forward, trap, and destroy the Soviet forces in the Don bend, and cover the Don River. They would be assisted by Romanian, Hungarian, and Italian forces. Kleist's First Panzer Army and General Richard Ruoff's Seventeenth Army would take Rostov. The First Panzer Army would then drive on the Caucasus oil fields, while the Seventeenth Army would take the Soviet ports on the Black Sea. The aim of the offensive was to take the oil fields in the Caucasus, thus giving Germany a new source of oil while depriving the Soviet Union of its major source of oil.[7]

For the upcoming offensive, only the divisions of Army Group South (divided into Army Groups A and B for the offensive) had to be completely rehabilitated. All of the panzer and motorized divisions in the southern Soviet Union were brought up to strength in men and equipment and even reinforced. Yet, even these preparations reveal the sad state of the German armed forces. For the Germans to reinforce their panzer and motorized divisions to the desired strength, OKH decided to rob Peter to pay Paul. The panzer divisions in Army Groups North and Center were ordered to give up one of their two tank battalions.[8] These would then go to either the panzer divisions in Army Groups A and B or to the motorized infantry divisions to give them some added punch. The 1st Panzer Division, for example, gave up the first battalion of its panzer regiment to the 16th Motorized Infantry Division in April 1942.[9]

All of the infantry divisions had to be brought up to strength in manpower and horses. Some 109,000 horses were brought in from Germany and another 188,000 from the occupied territories.[10] Even these, however, would not be enough. German horse requisitioning, in fact, would reach its height in 1942, with the Wehrmacht buying, requisitioning, or commandeering some 400,000 horses.[11] The majority of these were sent to Army Group South. Since Army Groups North and Center would be inactive, the horses in those sectors would be turned out to selected grazing areas during the spring and summer, while fodder was stockpiled for the next winter.[12]

The 1942 summer campaign began with the Soviets taking the initiative. Attacking out of the Izyum bulge on 12 May 1942, Marshal Semyon Timoshenko's southwest front sought to take Kharkov and destroy von Paulus's Sixth Army. The Germans were able to fend off the Soviet offensive after five dangerous days and, on 17 May, initiated their own offensive, with Kleist's First Panzer Army attacking north into the Soviet flank. The resulting encirclement yielded a bag of 214,000 prisoners, although the number of captured horses seems to have been rather small. The Sixth Army reported the capture by its infantry divisions of a total of 4,835 horses during the battle.[13] The First Panzer Army captured some 8,500 horses in the latter stages of the battle; these were divided among the XI, XLIV, and IV Romanian Corps.[14] This, along with Field Marshal Erich von Manstein's brilliant operations in the Crimea and the subsequent capture of Sebastopol, set the stage for the German summer offensive of 1942.

The German offensive (codenamed "Blue") jumped off on 28 June. The First Panzer Army and the Seventeenth Army were able to take Rostov quickly and then begin the drive to the Caucasus and the Black Sea coast. The Fourth Panzer and Sixth Armies drove forward into the Don bend, attempting to trap the Soviet forces between the Don and Donets rivers. They

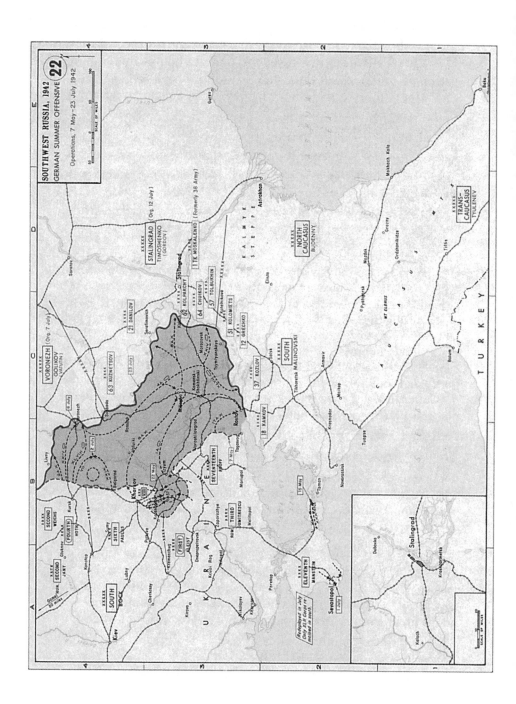

SOUTHWEST RUSSIA, 1942
GERMAN SUMMER OFFENSIVE **22**

Operations, 7 May – 23 July 1942

failed in this, however, and only a small bag of prisoners was taken. Liddell-Hart attributed this to an organizational change. As noted previously, during the fall and winter of 1941/42 all four of the panzer groups had been reorganized into panzer armies.[15] While this did make the panzer generals happy, as they now had equal status with their infantry counterparts, it also meant that these units incorporated a number of infantry divisions among their formations. This involved, as we have seen, providing an array of veterinary services for the infantry divisions. This, plus the inability of the infantry to keep pace with the panzers, tended to slow down the general tempo of the advance, which allowed the Soviets to escape.[16]

For the Germans, the 1942 campaign had many of the same frustrating features as the 1941 campaign, plus one additional frustration: to exploit the oil of the Caucasus fields, several agencies, including Göring's Four Year Plan, created a corporation, *Kontinentale Ol Aktiengesellschaft.* The actual operation of the oil fields was to be left to paramilitary organizations called Technical Brigades for Mineral Oil, or TBMs.[17] These units were sent to the minor oil field at Maikop after the First Panzer Army captured it on 15 August 1942. Once there, they found that the Soviets had thoroughly demolished the installations. Repair work proceeded at a slow pace, so that oil production began only in December, and with a daily output of only seventy barrels per day.[18] Shortly thereafter, the Soviet counteroffensive forced the Germans away from Maikop. The major fields at Grozny and Baku remained in Soviet hands throughout.

In terms of horses, the 1942 campaign bore a striking resemblance to the 1941 campaign. Although the general horse situation remained good, problems similar to those encountered in 1941 crept up once again. As in the 1941 campaign, the heavier western breeds suffered greatly. All of the divisions in the VIII Corps, for example, were suffering shortages of the heavier "troop" horses used to haul artillery. Although large numbers of panje horses were available, they were not capable of hauling guns.[19] In these circumstances, some infantry divisions "motorized" their artillery by using tractors commandeered from the numerous collective farms.[20] Once again, German equipment proved too heavy for horses to draw comfortably over long distances. Nevertheless, by 28 July the Sixth Army's ration strength was given as 400,000 men and 90,000 horses.[21]

As the summer wore on, however, and the Sixth Army crossed the Don to take Stalingrad, the situation changed. The taking of Stalingrad, once considered a minor objective, now assumed primary importance as it had become a contest between the wills of Hitler and Stalin, to the point where Hitler took units away from Kleist's front to feed them into the Stalingrad battle.[22] Since the Germans were condemned to fighting a static battle in a large city, units had to remain relatively stationary. This created a serious problem with fodder. The situation would have been even worse had not the Germans captured the grain elevator after hard fighting on 20 September 1942. The elevator was almost filled to capacity when captured. Several units requisitioned grain from the elevator for several weeks thereafter to feed their horses.[23]

Since formations remained stationary over an extended period of time, local sources of fodder were eventually exhausted. This meant that fodder had to be shipped by rail to Sixth Army units. In addition, the Third and Fourth Romanian Armies also required rather extensive amounts of fodder for their horses, and this also had to be sent in by rail.

Once again, as in 1941, the German Army was hamstrung by a lack of rail capacity. Rail communications beyond the Donets and south of the Don were sparse to begin with. As always, the Germans could not convert the few rail lines in the area rapidly enough or get them operating at a high capacity. By 21 October, the Sixth Army was dependent for supplies on a single track rail line that ran for some fifty miles from Debalzevo to Tschir. Because of high expenditures, artillery and 210mm mortar ammunition were in short supply. This meant that these bulky items got priority in the limited rail space available, producing a fodder crisis with the onset of autumn. Local fodder supplies had been exhausted. Grazing the horses on the steppe grasses was a suitable alternative, but only temporarily, as the grass would no longer be available after the first snowfall.[24]

Given this situation, the Sixth Army command decided that the majority of horses would be sent out of Stalingrad. Most of the Sixth Army's veterinary units would be sent to the rear. They would then be located on collective or state farms, where they would set up convalescent homes for the horses. Farms were the best sources of fodder and shelter for the coming winter.[25] The capacity of a convalescent home was originally set at 600, but by 14 September 1942 was expanded to between 1,200 and 1,500 horses.[26] The majority of the horses had been evacuated by the end of October.

Even with these measures, the horse situation in Stalingrad steadily worsened. By 9 November 1942 the quartermaster of the Sixth Army was reporting that hard fodder was still urgently needed. Casualties from exhaustion had almost doubled, with daily losses reaching 230.[27] This led the Sixth Army to consider evacuating even more horses by mid-November.[28] The operation was never carried out.

The evacuation of horses from Stalingrad is interesting on three counts: First, there is the standard argument that Hitler should have ordered the withdrawal of the Sixth Army from the city when it became apparent that a Soviet counteroffensive was imminent.[29] Such a withdrawal, however, could not have been accomplished quickly once the majority of the horses had been sent away. From the middle of October on, the Sixth Army was in effect immobilized operationally from lack of transport.

Another curious effect was that the battle of Stalingrad, ultimately, was not terribly hard on the German Army's stock of horseflesh. As noted previously, horse casualties from enemy action and exhaustion had mounted during the summer and autumn, with exhaustion becoming more serious during the autumn. With the evacuation, however, there were only about 25,000 horses in the city when the Soviet counteroffensive encircled the Sixth Army in the city on 23 November 1942.[30]

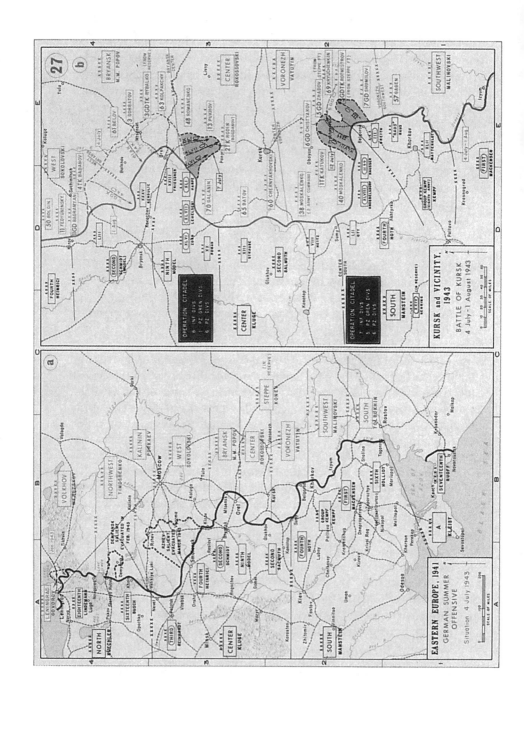

KURSK and VICINITY, 1943

BATTLE OF KURSK
4 July–1 August 1943

EASTERN EUROPE, 1941

GERMAN SUMMER OFFENSIVE

Situation 4 July 1943

Finally, if one takes a look at the Soviet situation at this time, some alarming trends were becoming evident, from the German point of view. According to a 1943 Soviet General Staff study, the Soviets had amassed for the Stalingrad counteroffensive some 719,702 men, 6,200 guns, and 1,510 tanks under the southwest, Don, and Stalingrad fronts. These three fronts required a total of some 169,609 horses for horse-drawn transportation.[31] Included in this total were the 42,249 horses of the IV, VIII, and III Guards Cavalry Corps.[32] These numbers are interesting for several reasons: First, they indicate how well the Soviet rail system was able to serve the Soviet Army, since the Soviets were operating under the same conditions as the Germans concerning fodder. Also, during the days of the German high tide in the summer, the Sixth Army alone required 90,000 horses for transportation.[33] Thus, it was evident even then that the Soviet Army was becoming more motorized, while the Wehrmacht was remaining stagnant at best in motorization. Finally, the Soviets were able to reduce their reliance on horses for transportation by steadily shrinking the size of their divisions. According to Foreign Armies East, the Soviet rifle division in the summer of 1942 contained some 15,534 men and employed 2,128 horses.[34] This was already a considerable reduction from the 1941 division. By December 1942 the division had shrunk even further, to a very lean 9,354 men, 44 guns, and 1,732 horses.[35]

After the Sixth Army, along with elements of the Fourth Panzer Army and the Third and Fourth Romanian Armies, was cut off in Stalingrad, a relief attempt was organized under von Manstein's command. While von Manstein would mount the relief effort with the newly organized Army Group Don, the pocket would have to be supplied by air. The Sixth Army estimated its daily requirements at about 600 tons of supplies. Although the Luftwaffe's capacity at best was only about 350 tons, Luftwaffe chief Göring, seeking to regain some of his lost standing with Hitler, promised to meet the Sixth Army's needs. In fact, the highest amount of supplies brought into Stalingrad on any one day was 300 tons, and this figure was achieved only three times during the entire airlift.[36] The supplies delivered consisted primarily of ammunition and some food. The soldiers in Stalingrad had to be put on short rations.

Given this situation, the 25,000 horses in Stalingrad represented two different things to the soldiers there. Given the rapidly dwindling supply of fodder, the horses that would otherwise become a liability could instead be used for food. By slaughtering the horses for meat, food supplies could be extended. This had been done successfully in 1941. Some horses had already been sent to the butcher as early as late November.[37]

On the other hand, the relief attempt was also to involve a breakout by the Sixth Army.[38] Von Paulus understood this as well. But if the Sixth Army was to break out, it would need the horses for transport. Army Group Don noted that the Sixth Army had some, 7,300 troop horses and 15,000 other horses in the city. Saving the troop horses was regarded as vital, since they would be needed to save at least some of the artillery. Therefore, Army Group Don requested that part of the daily air supply include twenty-two tons of fodder.[39] Given that the average supply tonnage delivered to Stalingrad daily was about 100 tons, this would have meant that over 20 percent of the supplies delivered would be fodder.[40] Despite this request, there seems to be no evidence from the available documents that any fodder was ever flown into the pocket. The quartermaster war diary of the Sixth Army contains inventories of what was brought into the city daily, but it never mentions fodder.[41] Even if the request for fodder was met, it would only have come to about six pounds per horse per day, still well below the amount of food required by a horse on a daily basis.

Preparations for the relief attempt also included supplying the beleaguered Sixth Army. The Fourth Panzer Army's columns were to carry some 600 tons of food for the Sixth Army. Also loaded in the Fourth Panzer Army's trucks were 200 tons of fodder for the horses.[42]

In the end, however, von Manstein's December relief effort was fended off by the Soviets. Most of the horses in Stalingrad were slaughtered for meat in large numbers beginning in mid-

January.[43] Some officers who had personal mounts, such as Colonel Doctor Herbert Rentsch, veterinary officer of the 94th Infantry Division, turned them loose rather than slaughter them, in the hope that some kindly Soviets might take them.[44] Von Paulus reported that the last horses had been eaten by 19 January 1943.[45] The final surrender took place on 2 February.

The battle of Stalingrad had been a disaster. About 147,000 German soldiers had been killed.[46] Although some 40,000 wounded and technical specialists had been flown out of the pocket by the air lift, 91,000 men, including von Paulus, who had been promoted to field marshal by Hitler in the expectation that he would shoot himself, had surrendered.[47] Huge numbers of guns, trucks, and other equipment had been lost. Oddly enough, the battle was not particularly hard on horses, as so many had been evacuated before the Sixth Army's encirclement. The same was true of the Sixth Army's veterinary units. Many of those had been moved back already and thus escaped the disaster.

In the south things were somewhat better. Given the more mobile nature of the campaign, fodder was less of a problem, since units were spread over a wide area. As the First Panzer Army began to outrun its supplies, horses had to be used to haul supplies. The quartermaster of the First Panzer Army made it quite clear that the needs of the army took priority over those of local agriculture.[48] As the tide turned, and events at Stalingrad threatened the positions of the First Panzer and Seventeenth Armies, an extended retreat over a long distance had to be conducted. This involved bringing a large number of tanks, trucks, guns, and other vehicles and equipment from advanced positions in the Caucasus back to Rostov for the First Panzer Army. The Seventeenth Army, along with elements of the First Panzer Army, retreated back to the Taman Peninsula, from which the army could retreat back across the Kerch Straits to the Crimea.

This retreat also involved the evacuation of horses. While in control of the area, the Germans made fairly extensive surveys of the available agricultural resources, including the number of pigs, cattle, sheep, and, of course, horses.[49] When the retreat began the Germans, aside from evacuating equipment, also evacuated horses, which they could not only use but at the same time deny to the Soviets. Although no figures are available for the First Panzer Army, when the Seventeenth Army retreated from the Taman Peninsula to the Crimea, some 177,355 German soldiers along with 50,139 other Axis soldiers and 28,486 Russian auxiliaries, or "Hiwis," were evacuated. Also evacuated were 21,230 motor vehicles, 1,815 guns, 27,741 wagons, and 72,899 horses.[50]

As stated previously, Stalingrad had not been particularly hard on the German Army's stock of horses, but the losses suffered in motor vehicles could not be made good by German industry. Through the first eight months of 1943, German truck production fell well short of the targets set for German industry. Especially large shortfalls were experienced in the production of trucks ranging from three to five tons. By August 1943, three-ton truck production amounted to 4,257 against a planned target of 6,677, a shortfall of 36.3 percent.[51] Allied bombing also had begun to seriously damage the Romanian oil industry. Romanian oil production declined in 1943 to 5,273,432 tons, which was only 45 percent of the planned production.[52] These conditions would necessitate an even greater dependence on horses.

Even while the Sixth Army was in its death throes, the Soviets were extending their offensive against the Germans. During January and February 1943, the Soviet winter offensive regained all of the territory lost during the summer but was unable to take Rostov before the First Panzer Army was able to escape from its exposed position in the Caucasus. As the Soviet offensive began to lose momentum from logistical difficulties toward the end of February, von Manstein, carefully husbanding a formidable force of panzer divisions, was able to launch a well-timed counteroffensive that drove the Soviets back to what had been the start line for the previous German summer offensive, except for a large bulge around the city of Kursk. This would be the focal point of operations for summer 1943.

The battle of Kursk occupies only a minor place in our story. Kursk was the largest tank battle in history, with the Germans throwing some 2,700 tanks in twelve panzer, six motorized infantry (now called panzer grenadier), and fifteen infantry divisions, supported by 1,830 aircraft in an offensive against both sides of the bulge.[53] Opposing them were some 4,000 Soviet tanks, supported by thick, well-sited lines of antitank guns and artillery, covered by hundreds of thousands of mines. Given that only fifteen infantry divisions were earmarked for the German offensive, the Germans employed only a relatively limited number of horses in comparison with their earlier offensive operations. Colonel General (later Field Marshal) Walter Model's Ninth Army, which was to employ some nineteen divisions in the offensive, including eight infantry divisions and one assault division, assembled some 50,000 horses, roughly about 6,000 horses for each infantry division, while the 78th Assault Division would use only 2,000 horses.[54] The Fourth Panzer Army quartermaster put the number of horses required by the Army at 25,000.[55] This number was reached by 3 June 1943.[56] As for the battle itself, horse casualties were rather minor. The Ninth Army, for example, suffered 5,981 horse casualties, including 3,107 killed, but that was for the entire month of July.[57]

With the failure of the German offensive, officially abandoned by Hitler's order on 13 July, the initiative passed to the Soviets for good. In the ensuing summer and autumn of 1943, the Soviets, under the direction of Zhukov, launched a series of offensives primarily against Army Group South. These operations drove the Germans back across the Ukraine. Army Group South was placed in grave danger in September, when the Soviet offensive threatened to beat the German retreat to the Dnepr, but was able to get across the river before the Soviets could get behind them.[58]

Normally, the autumn brings operations to a halt, as movement becomes extremely difficult during the muddy period. The Soviets, however, launched a series of offensives in October that breached the line of the Dnepr in more places than Army

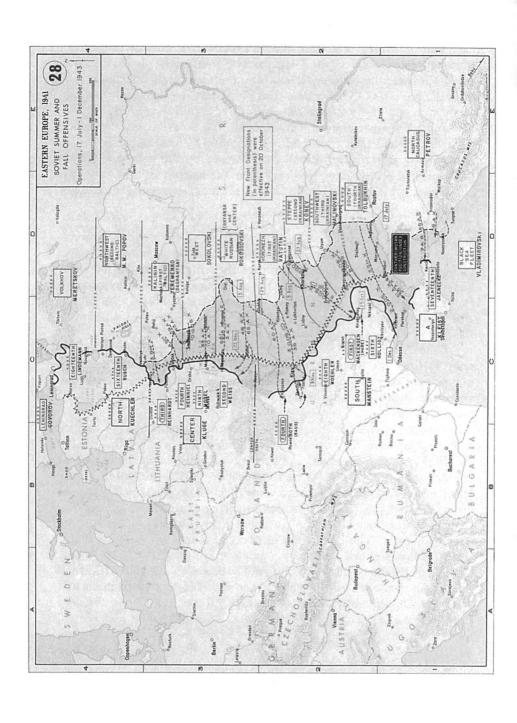

EASTERN EUROPE, 1941
SOVIET SUMMER AND
FALL OFFENSIVES
Operations, 17 July-1 December 1943

28

New Front Designations
(in parenthesis) were
effective on 20 October
1943

Group South could plug up. Further advances drove the Germans away from the river, and with the capture of Melitopol on 23 October, the German Seventeenth Army was effectively stranded in the Crimea. The offensive continued on into November, and Kiev was taken on 6 November. The Soviets were eventually brought to a halt by a counterattack mounted by von Manstein in late November and early December. Nonetheless, by the end of 1943, the Germans had been pushed well back from the Dnepr, with the exception of a salient held by Army Group South near the river around the town of Korsun.

The retreat was a difficult one for the horses. Although fodder was generally available, as the Germans retreated toward their supply sources, enemy artillery did cause some casualties. The constant movements also took their toll in terms of exhaustion. Particularly affected were the heavier "troop" horses, usually the more delicate western breeds. Although there were some shortages in numbers of horses, the Eighth Army reported no impairment of the marching ability of its divisions.[59] In some cases the Germans had surpluses of horses. The veterinary officer of the First Panzer Army reported that the remnants of divisions that were formed into "consolidated divisions" left these units with more horses than they could use. Surplus horses were to be released to the veterinary officer of the Sixth Army, and then turned out for agricultural work.[60]

In conducting their evacuations, the Germans usually tried to remove just about anything they could. In the Ukraine, this involved the evacuation of population, livestock, and agricultural equipment. Anything that could not be moved was to be destroyed.[61] During the retreat in the Ukraine, the Germans evacuated some 600,000 people, 268,000 tons of grain, and 488,000 head of livestock.[62] During Army Group Center's retreat to the Panther Line in August, the Army Group evacuated some 300,000 horses.[63] These activities in Army Group South were used after the war to prosecute von Manstein as a war criminal.

These evacuations, however, were not as thorough as the Germans had intended. Evacuation efforts were met with widespread propaganda and sabotage. Consequently, when the Soviets crossed the Dnepr, the area they had just taken still contained some 2,987,699 cattle and horses, many of which probably wound up in Soviet Army units, as did the 80,000 men drafted by the Soviet Army from the towns, villages, and cities taken by them so recently.[64]

The wanton destructiveness of the German retreat, aside from displaying the German talent for demolition, also clearly demonstrated the depth to which Germany's military fortunes had sunk. Victory, the hopes of which had appeared so certain in the days of high summer in 1942, was now an impossibility. Pressed back in the east by increasingly superior Soviet forces, clinging tenaciously to the Gustav Line in Italy, under increasing pressure from the air, defeated at sea, and anxiously awaiting the Allied invasion of France, Hitler's Germany was now careening out of control toward inevitable disaster.

A German 105mm artillery battalion on the march in Russia during the 1941 campaign. NATIONAL ARCHIVES

Regiment "Doberritz" on a prewar parade through a German town. Note that the officers are mounted. U.S. ARMY WAR COLLEGE

Mountain troops on an exercise in the Bavarian Alps before the war. Note the mules. Mules, a rarity in Germany, were normally assigned exclusively to specialized units such as Mountain troops. U.S. ARMY WAR COLLEGE

A Russian panje cart being drawn by two panje horses. Although the photograph was taken in 1941, this vehicle remained a major form of transport for both the German and Soviet armies throughout the war.

A German remount commission buying horses in a French town in the autumn of 1949. NATIONAL ARCHIVES

A veterinarian draws blood from a horse. Such examinations were administered periodically to horses as a preventative measure against contagious disease. NATIONAL ARCHIVES

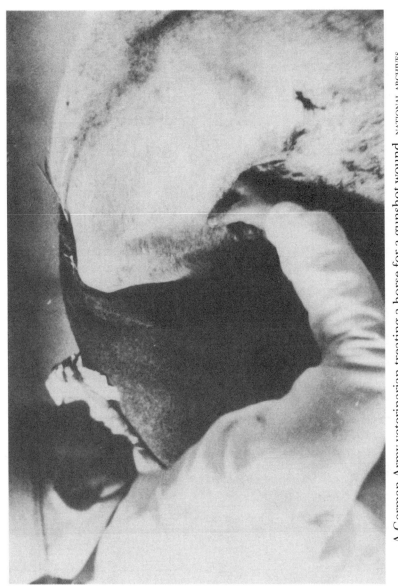

A German Army veterinarian treating a horse for a gunshot wound. NATIONAL ARCHIVES

Nonambulatory horse casualties being loaded into a special vehicle to carry them to a veterinary station. This picture was taken near Abbeville in June 1940. NATIONAL ARCHIVES

Draft horses fording a river during the 1940 campaign. In this case, the horses were tied to pneumatic rafts and swam across. NATIONAL ARCHIVES

Hard-riding troopers of the 1st Cavalry Division fording the Semois River in Belgium, May 1940.

CHAPTER 5

Germany and the Occupied Territories

Some infantry divisions had been in France since 1940, and had been used to train replacements for the east or south. They had a hard core of experienced officers and non-commissioned officers, but many had been wounded and were not completely fit for active duty.

Friedrich Ruge[1]

The exceptionally heavy bombing attacks which the English have launched against the western lines of communication for some days are rather suspicious. Could it be that this is the prelude to an attempt at invasion?

Joseph Goebbels, 10 September 1943[2]

Here I must make a necessary digression from the main thread of this book. When the Nazi empire reached its territorial height in September 1942, Germany controlled Europe from the Volga in the east to the Pyrenees in the west, and from Norway in the north to North Africa in the south. All of these areas, with the exception of North Africa, if not the scene of active operations, required garrison forces at the very least. These forces also made extensive use of horses and must be looked at, if only briefly. Also, we must look at conditions in Germany itself during the war, including some interesting experiments in horse breeding. Finally, we will also examine the campaign in Italy from the initial Allied invasion on 8 September 1943 until the spring of 1944.

To the German Army, France represented many different things. It was a source of valuable raw material and slave labor for German factories. France also provided a quiet area where shattered divisions could be rebuilt. Finally, France was a valuable source of horseflesh. By as early as 28 February 1942, occupied France had delivered 153,000 horses, as well as vast amounts of fodder, to the Wehrmacht.[3] German units, when sent back from the Soviet Union, brought their horses with them. Once in France, any horse judged no longer fit for military service would be unloaded.[4] This usually was done by selling them off to French peasants at remount markets, where indigenous horses would be purchased by the army.[5]

While in France, divisions often served as pools from which horses could be drawn by divisions that were due to be sent to the eastern front. During the second half of April 1942, for example, the 370th and 371st Infantry Divisions were in the process of completing their training before being sent to the Soviet Union for the ill-fated summer campaign of 1942.[6] During this period, the 370th Infantry Division received some 1,570 horses from the 302nd Infantry Division, while the 371st Infantry Division obtained 554 horses from the 711th Infantry Division.[7]

Quiet areas such as Norway also provided places where shattered or destroyed divisions could be refitted or rebuilt. This was especially true after Stalingrad, where twenty German divisions were lost. These divisions were resupplied with manpower from several sources, primarily the division's replacement battalion back in Germany. Also, the standard German Army personnel policy was to always return wounded soldiers to their old units after their recovery.[8] Finally, personnel were saved when some 40,000 men were flown out of the pocket during the airlift.[9]

The veterinary personnel of the infantry divisions was largely unaffected by the Stalingrad disaster. Since most of the horses had been evacuated before November, the veterinary units of most of the Sixth Army's infantry divisions had also been pulled out of the city to staff the convalescent homes for the horses, and thus were able to avoid encirclement in Stalingrad. The 295th Infantry Division, for example, had sent its veterinary company back to Dnepropetrovsk to operate a convalescent home and thus could be sent back to the division when it was rebuilt in Norway.[10]

Units rebuilding in occupied territories generally obtained horses locally. Units in Norway, however, had to have their horses shipped to them, as Norway did not have a large horse population. That the Wehrmacht was dependent on horses for transport is clearly indicated in the horse population statistics of Germany and the occupied countries. Clearly, the two hardest hit areas were the Soviet Union and Poland. At the height of its power, Germany controlled an area of the Soviet Union that contained about 11 million horses. Of these, some 7 million were "killed or taken away" during the war.[11]

Poland was even more seriously affected. Right from the first, Poland was expected to provide large numbers of horses for the German Army.[12] Throughout the war, Poland was ruthlessly stripped of horses. Between 1939 and 1945, Poland's horse population declined by about 36 percent, from 3,914,000 to 1,395,000.[13]

Another favored source of horseflesh was Hungary. Large numbers of horses were purchased from Hungary, especially for the 1940 campaign. Although German soldiers were skeptical at first because of their appearance, the endurance and fine performance of Hungarian horses in the campaign convinced any doubters as to their usefulness.[14]

The western European countries also contributed their share to the German Army's stock of horses. Holland's heavy farm horses were valuable as draft horses for the artillery.[15] As such they were heavily utilized. One author has claimed that the number of draft horses on farms in Holland actually increased during the war, owing to a shortage of tractors.[16] This assertion is clearly refuted, however, by official Dutch statistics. From 1940 to 1945, the number of horses registered for work in agriculture declined from 326,000 to 302,000, a decrease of about 9 percent.[17]

France and Germany also suffered decreases in horse population, but losses and heavy requisitions were offset to some degree by horses sold by the army back to the civilian population. Nonetheless, during the war Germany began to experience a shortage of horses, with the shortfall becoming pronounced by mid-1944.[18]

Matters were made worse because Germany's industry could not make good the losses suffered in motor vehicles in the Soviet Union and North Africa during 1941 and 1942. After the disasters at Stalingrad and in North Africa, Germany would be faced with shortages of vehicles, oil, and drivers. These shortfalls could only be made up by the even more extensive use of horses.[19]

Given these circumstances, the German Army sought to economize on its use of horses in various ways. First, a number of divisions in western Europe were assigned to the defense of Hitler's so-called Atlantic Wall. These units, such as the 709th and 716th Infantry Divisions, were placed in sectors near the coast. The artillery of these divisions was placed in concrete emplacements along the coast. While this obviated the need for horses to haul the guns about, it also left these divisions poorly prepared for any kind of operation other than static defense.[20]

The German Army also began to vary the organizations used in its infantry divisions. The divisional organization adopted by the infantry branch on 5 November 1943 was not uniformly applied throughout the army. Nonetheless, German infantry divisions in general were now reduced by three infantry battalions.[21] The reduction of divisions by about one infantry regiment produced a saving of 641 horses.[22] Further savings were created by cuts in the divisional artillery. Also, by the latter stages of the war, the army had abandoned the heavy steel vehicles with which it began the war and by now had gone to using wooden carts often drawn by single horses, although this would cause problems of a different sort, as shall be seen.

Horses with units in occupied countries also had to receive the most thorough care possible. This involved the careful stocking of feed during the summer and fall for the oncoming winter. For the winter, units were issued precise instructions early for building special stalls to provide warmth for horses. These stalls could be located in existing buildings. Good overhead cover and thick straw matting on the walls for insulation was especially demanded.[23]

Yet, while the Germans could conserve horseflesh effectively, they could (and did) waste it as well. The best example of this was the raising of the Luftwaffe field divisions. Mounting losses in aircraft left the Luftwaffe with large numbers of surplus ground personnel. These men represented a potentially valuable source of replacements for the army. The corpulent Luftwaffe chief, however, was unwilling to place his dedicated National Socialists in the army's decadent clutches.[24] Instead, the Luftwaffe began deploying Luftwaffe field divisions in late 1942 and deployed twenty-one such divisions by 1 July 1943.[25]

Since motor vehicles and gasoline were in short supply, horses had to be used to provide some transport for these divisions. By 1944 they had an authorized horse strength of 1,263.[26] These divisions proved to be of almost no use in combat. Having little training and in many cases with no experienced cadres, they tended to disintegrate immediately upon their entry into combat. Even worse, these units often used highly skilled technicians as combat troops, which vitiated Germany's ability to expand and maintain aircraft production.[27] After the initial failure of these divisions in the field, they were still maintained, even though Luftwaffe officers thought them a poor idea.[28] In fact, the army had to provide them with officers and noncommissioned officers (NCOs) to give them some rudimentary training. Eventually, sanity prevailed and most of these formations were broken up after October 1943.[29] Nonetheless, as late as 31 July 1944, the Germans still had eleven of these formations on the books or in the field.[30] Since these divisions also employed horses, these units wasted both men and horses in a profligate fashion.

In addition to the Soviet front, Germany became involved in two other campaigns in Europe between 1942 and 1944. The first was in the air. Germany now became subject to the attentions of the American Eighth and Fifteenth Air Forces and RAF Bomber Command, as called for in the directive of Operation Pointblank, presented on 10 June 1943. Although involving huge numbers of men and large amounts of materiel, the strategic bombing campaign figures very little in our study. Even at the height of the bombing in the summer of 1944, losses of horses from bombing were negligible, reaching a high of only 111 in August 1944.[31]

After clearing North Africa in May 1943, the Allies invaded Sicily in July. This campaign does not really concern us, as the German defense was conducted by four mobile divisions, all of which successfully escaped to the Italian mainland. Following this, the Allies invaded Italy on 8 September 1943, advancing slowly up the peninsula until they were halted at the German positions at Cassino in the Gustav Line.

Although the Italian campaign will not occupy a major part of this book, it deserves some attention for several reasons: First, it provides a good example of how the German Army improvised to give formations some degree of motorization in their transportation. In Italy, the Germans used the Ansaldo-Fiat works to produce various types of vehicles, including even assault guns and reconnaissance cars. These vehicles were sent to units that were either in Italy or in the Balkans.[32]

As far as the use of animals is concerned, the interesting thing here was the heavy reliance on mules and donkeys for transport. By 1 January 1944, the Tenth Army had 26,212 animals, of which some 7,409 (28 percent) were mules and donkeys.[33] Since the Tenth Army was directly responsible for the defense of the key sectors of Cassino and Anzio, the Tenth Army got the majority of the mules. The Fourteenth Army, holding the eastern part of the Gustav Line, had far fewer mules and donkeys. By 1 January 1944, the Fourteenth Army employed only 982 mules out of a total of 21,592 animals.[34] For the German forces in Italy, mules were undoubtedly obtained locally, as mules were rarely bred in Germany.[35]

Another interesting facet of the Italian campaign was that the Allies were also constrained to use animals for transport. The Allies had discovered the need for animal transport as early as the Sicilian campaign, when Major General Lucian Truscott's 3rd Infantry Division employed over 500 mules and pack horses in its advance over Sicily's mountainous terrain.[36] When the mainland was invaded, Fifth Army commander General Mark Clark quickly saw how valuable mules and horses could be in terrain unsuited to motor vehicles.[37] By May 1944 the Fifth Army's remount service had grown to 15,000 horses and mules. Since veterinarians and other personnel were scarce, the remount service was staffed by Italian personnel. Equipment for the horses and mules was made locally.[38]

The German Army used many different breeds of horses. As such, each breed had its strengths and weaknesses. Cold bloods, while being very strong physically, were very sensitive to extremes of temperature, had special diet problems, and tended to be slow moving. Warm bloods, although livelier and faster with more endurance than cold bloods, lacked their strength for hauling heavy equipment. Also, some breeds were more specialized for draft work, while others were suitable only for riding purposes.

Given this problem, the German Army, or rather the Inspectorate of Riding and Driving to be specific, tried to develop an all-around military horse. Experiments in cross-breeding were conducted at the army remount depot at Grabau-Schönböken. The goal was to develop a new type of mixed blood horse that could satisfy both military and civilian needs, combining the strength of a cold blood with the lively temperament of a warm blood.[39]

Symptomatic of the Nazi penchant for bureaucratic conflict, the Security Service (SD) also conducted breeding experiments to develop the same type of horse.[40]

In both cases, the experiments failed. The military experiments made some progress, but had far too little time to be able to reach a successful conclusion. Burkhart Müller-Hillebrand, however, felt that eventually the army would have developed a good all-around horse.[41] The SD's breeding experiments failed utterly. Attempts were made to breed work horses with warm blood studs and cold blood mares, but the resulting offspring were too weak. Slightly better results were obtained using the combination of cold blood studs and warm blood mares. The government did create studding stations, but the studs became so overworked and strained that they could not sire offspring.[42]

In any case, the days of "quiet" sectors were over. For with the coming of spring in 1944, the Wehrmacht would find itself pressed not only in the east and in Italy, but would now have to face the greatest amphibious invasion in history.

CHAPTER 6

Jine the Cavalry

Jine the cavalry . . .
American Civil War song
The golden age of cavalry and moving artillery with horse traction is past, that is an undeniable fact.
Anonymous, 1937[1]

The cavalry must be capable of the conduct of *independent* operations and thereby decisive battle. To this end, the creation of a Cavalry Corps of 2–3 divisions is required. That is the only reason for the existence of the cavalry.
Kurt Feldt, 13 August 1940[2]

From these experiences the Cavalry Division proposes: conversion of the Cavalry Division to a Panzer Division.
Kurt Feldt, 13 September 1941[3]

One of the oldest relationships in war is that shared between a cavalryman and his horse. Inseparable companions, a good cavalryman generally takes better care of his mount than of his wife. Thus, this book would not be complete without a look at Germany's employment of cavalry.

Like all the other major European powers, Germany's record in its employment of cavalry in World War I was mixed. Theoretically, cavalry was the mobile element of the armies of 1914. However, given the amount of rail capacity required to keep a cavalry division in the field, as pointed out by Norman Stone, cavalry often impaired an army's mobility as much as it enhanced it.[4]

On the western front, the use of cavalry quickly became impractical, owing to the relatively constricted length of the front and the deadly realities of trench warfare. In the east, however, where the trench lines were not so thick and the front extended over thousands of miles, cavalry could still be employed with some degree of effectiveness. In late November 1914, for example, German cavalry brilliantly covered the retreat of General Scheffer's reserve corps, helping to save it from almost certain destruction.[5]

As in other European armies, the cavalry branch in Germany had a fair amount of clout. The Reichswehr, although a small force, had three cavalry divisions.[6] The cavalry also maintained its aura of being an elite branch. Colonel Hans von Luck recalled his bitter disappointment at being transferred from a cavalry regiment to a newly formed motorized battalion.[7]

During the interwar years, the same question that plagued the British Army tormented the Germans as well. Did the cavalry have a role in an army where the possibilities of mechanization and motorization existed? In Germany, as in Britain, the development of armored formations was resisted by the cavalry, which saw its traditional role being usurped by a bunch of upstarts. In Germany, the creation of the panzer force really came out of experiments with motorized supply units, conducted by Guderian and his protectors, Generals Oswald Lutz and Erich von Tschischwitz.[8]

The cavalry, however, had its defenders. Foremost among these was General Maximilian von Poseck, who had been chief of the Cavalry Inspectorate during the 1920s.[9] Von Poseck vigorously argued for the cavalry in the pages of the standard German military periodical, *Militär Wochenblatt*. In one article, Poseck argued that cavalry had greater cross-country mobility than motorized units, which he depicted as being primarily bound to good roads.[10] Later on he argued that cavalry and armored vehicles could work together in combined units.[11] These ideas were ruthlessly shot down by Guderian, who fought for both motorization and mechanization.[12]

The tank enthusiasts won, however, due in no small part to the fact that the development of the panzer arm was clearly supported by Hitler, who was strongly attracted to what were then considered novel forms of warfare.[13] Also important was the general open-mindedness of German officers to new ideas. Even an old-timer such as von Rundstedt, who once told Guderian that his ideas were nonsense, quickly changed his mind when showed the tank's true potential and arguably became Germany's best practitioner of mobile warfare.[14] This attitude was reflected by many other cavalry officers who transferred to the panzer arm. It is interesting to note that many of the finer German tank commanders, including Kleist, Hasso von Manteuffel, and Mackensen to name a few, were originally cavalrymen.[15] This was in striking contrast to the British Army, where the attempt to convert cavalry units to tanks generally produced lamentable results.[16]

The cavalry branch suffered an irreparable blow to its position when in 1938 it was replaced by the Inspectorate of Riding and Driving as the ultimate authority on equine matters.[17] Observing the trends, the cavalry got involved in the motorization program. The outcome was the conversion of two cavalry divisions into two of the four light divisions.[18] These were built around two *Kavallerie-Schützen* regiments, each of two battalions, plus a tank battalion equipped with only Pz I and Pz II light tanks.[19] Before the war, Guderian was critical of these formations, arguing that they were insufficiently equipped with tanks and thus had only a limited capability to undertake offensive operations.[20] The panzer leader's criticism was proven correct in the Polish campaign.[21] After their poor performance in Poland, the light divisions were upgraded to panzer divisions in the fall and winter of 1939/40.

As for the more traditional horse cavalry, a brigade was employed in Poland. The 1st Cavalry Brigade's mission in Poland was to cover the left flank of the Third Army as it moved south from East Prussia.[22] In fact, von Rundstedt lamented that the German Army did not use more cavalry in Poland. He felt

that Poland's geography was eminently suitable for the employment of cavalry and could have been well used in its traditional
screening role.[23]

In any case, for the invasion of Western Europe in 1940,
the horse cavalry presence in the German Army was expanded
to a division of two brigades. The unit, commanded by Major
General Kurt Feldt, was employed in the Eighteenth Army's
drive across Holland. The division's after-action report noted
that during the first phase of the German offensive in May
1940, the division could play but only a minor role in the operation. Holland, with its numerous water obstacles and polder-
land, was poorly suited to the employment of cavalry.[24] During
the final German offensive in June, the 1st Cavalry Division was
placed behind Hoth's panzer divisions and eventually took
part in the overrunning of Normandy. During these operations, the cavalry again played very little of an active role. General Fridolin von Senger und Etterlin, who commanded one of
the division's two brigades, noted that his brigade, despite all
efforts, failed to reach the front in time to participate in major
combat operations.[25] Feldt noted in the division's after-action
report that the basic problem was that the 1st Cavalry Division
was neither fish nor fowl. While its horse-based mobility made
it faster than an infantry division, it lacked the speed and
power of a panzer or motorized infantry formation. Thus, to
be used effectively, especially in the east, Feldt recommended
that a cavalry corps of two or three divisions be created.[26]

This was not destined to happen, however. While the number of panzer divisions was doubled, the single, solitary cavalry
division of the German Army remained just that—single and
solitary. The SS, however, did extemporize the SS Cavalry Brigade.[27] In any case, the Wehrmacht entered the Soviet Union
with less than nine thousand cavalry.

In the 1941 Soviet campaign, the cavalry was deployed as follows: The SS Cavalry Brigade, although not committed in the
initial advance, was inserted into the Soviet Union by August to
operate against any Soviet troops still at large behind German
lines.[28] The 1st Cavalry Division was attached to Army Group

Center. It was under the command of General Baron Leo Geyr von Schweppenburg's XXIV Panzer Corps, part of Guderian's Second Panzer Group.[29] During the campaign the 1st Cavalry Division performed the traditional cavalry duties of screening and reconnaissance, as well as providing flank protection for the panzer group. In addition, the division also operated in areas that were unsuited to motor vehicles, such as the northern edge of the huge Pripet Marsh.[30] Certainly the division performed its missions well. Guderian specifically mentioned the 1st Cavalry Division as a good fighting outfit.[31]

Nonetheless, losses were heavy. Between 22 June and 29 July 1941, the division suffered some 2,002 casualties, including 109 officers. Some squadrons had shrunk to 41 percent of their authorized strength. To be able to undertake further missions, the division required some 1,280 men and 1,435 horses, plus equipment, especially replacement parts for machine guns.[32]

The 1st Cavalry Division rested and refitted during the first two weeks of August. After that it was committed to the Gomel area, where it was involved in fending off an abortive Soviet attack against the flank of Guderian's thrust south against Kiev. Since the division was completely dependent upon horses, the usual problems with them were encountered, especially in the artillery. Here the division's problem was twofold: First, it lacked organic heavy artillery, a serious organizational deficiency. Second, the division's artillery horses were seriously affected by the nonstop tempo of operations, especially in the Gomel battles.[33]

By 13 September 1941, Feldt proposed to OKH that the 1st Cavalry Division be converted into a panzer division. He noted that while the division had been able to perform all of its assigned missions well, it could not play a decisive role in battle. Feldt also observed that other army groups, armies, and panzer groups did not have cavalry divisions and were able to do without them. He took this to mean that, while cavalry divisions could certainly be useful, they were not an essential requirement. In his report to OKH, Feldt also abandoned his notion of creating a cavalry corps of several divisions. In addition, he noted that certain elements of the division, such as headquarters, communications, engineers, antitank troops, and artillery required motor vehicles rather than horses for mobility. Given these circumstances, Feldt proposed that the 1st Cavalry Division be converted into a panzer division. For purposes of divisional integrity, he proposed that all of the division's units be involved in the division's conversion.[34] Feldt's wishes were granted, for in the autumn of 1941 the 1st Cavalry Division was converted into the 24th Panzer Division, with the changeover officially taking place on 1 December 1941.[35] In keeping with the cavalry origins of the new division, the officers and men retained their old uniforms, a decision that seemed to cause a tremendous amount of confusion for the tailors making German Army uniforms.[36] Von Senger und Etterlin noted with delight that the tactical sign of the 24th Panzer Division was a prancing horse.[37]

Although the army's only cavalry division was converted into a panzer division, the Germans continued to organize cavalry units. Many division commanders formed ad hoc cavalry squadrons for purposes of patrolling and reconnaissance.[38] The SS also deployed large cavalry units. The 8th SS Cavalry Division (*Florian Geyer*) became operational on 21 June 1942. Composed of two cavalry regiments, a horse-drawn artillery regiment, a motorcycle battalion, and a veterinary company, it had 159 officers, 819 NCOs and 4,400 men.[39] It was used primarily for antipartisan operations, and early on its units showed a penchant for committing atrocities.[40]

The Germans also organized cavalry units manned by people from the Soviet Union who were unhappy with Communist rule. The most notable was the Cossack division. The Cossacks were rather fortunate in their relations with the German Army in that they enjoyed a special status among the makers of occupation policy in Germany. In fact, they were not even classified as being *Untermensch*, a benefit rarely dispensed to the unfortunate people of the Soviet Union.[41] Large numbers of Cossacks were willing to volunteer their services to the Germans. In late 1942 the Germans formed a Cossack cavalry division, com-

manded by a German officer, General Hellmuth von Pannwitz.[42] Deemed fully operational on 1 August 1943, it was sent
to Yugoslavia to conduct antipartisan operations, at which it
was fairly successful.[43] In terms of horses, like all other Cossack
and Kalmuck cavalry formations, the men had to provide their
own mounts.[44] Once in Yugoslavia, however, they undoubtedly
would have had to rely on standard German Army supply channels for remounts and replacements. A second Cossack cavalry
division was formed in September 1944 and combined with the
original Cossack cavalry division to create a Cossack cavalry
corps, which spent the war in Yugoslavia.[45]

As the war dragged on, the German Army deployed more
and more cavalry. One recent author, noting that by the summer of 1944 the German Army had 95,000 cavalry, has argued
that this constituted some sort of backward step for the German Army.[46] I disagree with this assertion. Although the number 95,000 is a large one, this figure could only be reached if
one includes every kind of mounted soldier employed in the
German Army, including regular cavalry, antipartisan units,
and mounted police. For the German cavalry, horses were
strictly for mobility. German cavalry combat training stressed
fighting on foot, utilizing the standard principle of combined
arms.[47] Troopers were also given a great deal of training in elementary veterinary care for the horse.[48] Troopers were even
given training in horse holding, which was necessary when a
mounted unit went into action. The soldiers fought without
their horses, which were sent back, behind the lines, where
someone had been detailed to hold the horses' reins.[49] In
addition, cavalry could be very useful in certain roles, such as
antipartisan operations and for operating in marshy areas
unsuited to motor vehicles.

As 1944 wore on, the Germans were steadily pushed back
by the Soviets in the east. While Army Group South retreated
back toward the Romanian border, Army Group Center also
had to retreat and by the spring of 1944 found its right flank
anchored on the northern edge of the Pripet Marsh. In view of
the fact that the Germans would be operating in that area, the

German Cavalry Corps was officially established on 28 May 1944.[50] The corps was to be a small one in terms of cavalry, consisting of the German 4th Cavalry Brigade and the Hungarian 1st Cavalry Division, some infantry, and the 4th Panzer Division, plus some attached miscellaneous units. It was commanded by General Gustav Harteneck, and in fact its initial designation was *Gruppe Harteneck.*[51]

Problems were encountered even in the creation of the cavalry units for the corps. Since the cavalry units were horse cavalry, mounts had to be obtained. To accomplish this, during the winter units were ordered to provide horses to serve as mounts for the Cavalry Corps. In Army Group South, for example, the 34th, 75th, and 82nd Infantry Divisions were ordered by Army Group South to turn over some 250 horses to Army Group Center for the then forming Cavalry Corps.[52] These divisions, however, were caught up in the battle of Korsun pocket and could dispatch a total of only seventy horses by the end of February.[53] The situation did not improve in March either. A Soviet offensive forced the withdrawal of the 584th Horse Collection Station, which was handling the transfers. Thus, Army Group South's orders could not be fulfilled.[54]

Another problem encountered, at least in Harteneck's eyes, was the performance of the Hungarian 1st Cavalry Division. The division had evidently not performed well at all, and had been removed from the corps's order of battle by July.[55] The imminent return of the division to the corps at the beginning of August prompted a bitter letter from Harteneck to General Walter Weiss, the commander of the Second Army. Harteneck complained that Hungarian units tended to run away rather ingloriously. One regiment, he protested, was living on the reputation it had gained when once it launched a saber charge against the Russians. To arm them with German weapons, Harteneck wrote, was foolish because the Hungarians threw them away as quickly as they discarded Hungarian weapons. If they were to be employed at all, they would have to be corseted with strong German units. Ultimately, the only correct solution for the very agitated Harteneck was to send the entire Hungarian 1st Cavalry Division, as well as all other Hungarian troops, back to Hungary.[56] Harteneck apparently got his wish, as the matter does not appear in subsequent documents. Instead, a second German cavalry brigade, the 3rd, was formed and added to the corps at the beginning of August.[57]

Through the summer and autumn of 1944, the Cavalry Corps fought as part of the Second Army to stem the Soviet offensive that had obliterated Army Group Center. In the course of the fighting it suffered relatively light losses, although numerous other difficulties were encountered. The arrival of supply trains and horse transports were delayed by constant air attacks.[58] The 14,000 cavalry in the 3rd and 4th Cavalry Brigades also suffered from fodder and equipment shortages. Fodder was in short supply and the situation was made worse by the misuse and waste of fodder, a situation that unit commanders and their supply and veterinary officers were instructed to correct. The disposal of numerous animal corpses was also a problem.[59] The 4th Cavalry Brigade reported a shortage of harnesses. The entire corps was even short of riding breeches![60]

By the end of the war, most German cavalry units had disappeared. The 8th SS Cavalry Division was encircled and destroyed in Budapest in February 1945.[61] The Cossacks suffered perhaps the grimmest fate of all. Captured by the Allies, the Cossacks were turned back over to the tender mercies of Stalin's Soviet Union. Von Pannwitz was hanged by the Soviets as a war criminal on 16 January 1947.[62] As for the Cavalry Corps, as the front moved away from the Pripet Marsh, there was less and less reason for it, and, by the onset of the winter of 1944/45, one that had more infantry than cavalry at that. Thus, the Cavalry Corps was broken up at the end of 1944.[63] The German Cavalry Corps had preceded the Third Reich in its passage into history.

CHAPTER 7

Disaster and Defeat

> The battlefield at Falaise was unquestionably one of the greatest "killing grounds" of any of the war areas. Roads, highways and fields were so choked with destroyed equipment and with dead men and animals that passage through the area was extremely difficult.
>
> Dwight D. Eisenhower[1]

The year 1944 was one of unrelieved disaster for Germany. On all fronts the Wehrmacht was dealt a series of shattering blows, continuing through the end of 1944 right up until the final collapse of Nazi Germany. From the point of view of this book, the campaigns of 1944, particularly in France and Byelorussia, bring forth in sharp relief the shortcomings of the German Army in its reliance on horses.

The year began with a battle on the eastern front that threatened a major disaster for Army Group South and in fact turned out to be a minor disaster. On 25 January 1944, the Soviets, employing two tank armies and several other armies under the first and second Ukrainian fronts, attacked both sides of the base of the German salient near the Dnepr River. The Soviets' spearheads met on 28 January at Shpola, forming what would be called the Korsun pocket.[2] Trapped in the pocket were the XI and XLII Corps, comprised of the 57th, 72nd, 88th, and 289th Infantry Divisions, along with the 5th SS Panzer Division (*Viking*), the SS Walloon Brigade and Corps Group B, and an ad hoc formation consisting of the remnants of the 112th, 255th, and 332nd Infantry Divisions.[3] Total German strength in the pocket was about 56,000 men, the largest number encircled since Stalingrad.[4]

Throughout the last days of January and the first week of February, the battle raged as von Manstein mounted several relief operations, which the Soviets fended off with difficulty. Finally, having failed to relieve the pocket, von Manstein ordered a breakout on 10 February. Although the breakout succeeded, it did so at heavy cost. The number of men who did escape varies widely according to different sources. Soviet sources generally claim that the pocket was virtually wiped out.[5] A popular German source stated that 35,000 men escaped, a rather high figure.[6] A more accurate German source gives the number as being about 20,000.[7]

In any case, the breakout was a logistical disaster. The last obstacle the encircled *Gruppe Stemmermann* had to cross was a swift-running, deep and icy stream, the Gniloy Tikich. Under heavy artillery fire, the Germans had to abandon all of their heavy equipment. Although no numbers are available, all of the horses inside the pocket were lost, as they could not lord the Gniloy Tikich.[8]

After the battle of Korsun, Army Group South was driven back in a series of battles in the spring of 1944, which ultimately resulted in Hitler sacking two of his top commanders, von Manstein and von Kleist. What made these Soviet offensives even more unpalatable to the Germans was that the Soviets were able to undertake them during the spring, when operations were usually brought to a halt by the mud. The Soviets' ability to do this reflected their increasing level of motorization, brought about mainly by large numbers of American-made trucks. The Soviets also used, as did the Germans, the one-horse panje wagon, which was light enough to ride over the mud without getting stuck.[9] The German catalog of defeats in the spring was completed by a disaster in the Crimea, where Hitler's failure to order a timely evacuation cost the Germans some 80,000 killed, wounded, and captured.[10] To prevent their falling into Soviet hands during the final stages of the Seventeenth Army's debacle, the army's entire remaining stock of horses, some 30,000, were shot and thrown into the Bay of Severnaya.[11]

While the battles of early 1944 were being fought in the Ukraine and the Crimea, and the Allies broke through the Gustav Line in Italy, the German Army in the west awaited the expected Allied invasion of France. In this theater, German infantry divisions were beset with a variety of problems. The prime of these was mobility. The German Army in the west disposed of some 48 infantry divisions, but the mobility of these divisions varied widely. Some, such as the 77th, 84th, 85th, and 352nd Infantry Divisions, had their full complement of 300 motor vehicles. Others, such as the 272nd and 276th Infantry Divisions, although assigned between 200 and 300 trucks each, had only received between 50 and 80 each by May 1944.[12]

Fuel was also a problem. By 1944 Germany's oil situation was desperate. The oil campaign carried out by the Allied air forces in mid-1944 had greatly affected Germany's synthetic oil production.[13] Allied bombing attacks also seriously damaged the Romanian oil industry. Romanian oil production fell from 5,665,357 tons in 1942 to 5,273,432 tons in 1943, and then to only 3,525,000 tons in 1944.[14] Further difficulties were created when the British Royal Air Force (RAF) was able to disrupt oil traffic from Romania to Germany by heavily mining the Danube River.[15] The Germans ultimately lost their most important source of oil when Romania changed sides on 23 August 1944.

Since tanks and other armored fighting vehicles had to have priority for gasoline and diesel fuel, the Germans made efforts to save fuel used by trucks. The army, for example, attempted to adapt vehicles to run on wood gas. This effort, however, did not meet with success. On 29 May 1944 the quartermaster of Army Group B noted that of the 14,578 trucks in the Seventh and Fifteenth Armies, only 3,552 had been converted to run on wood gas. Tires were also in short supply.[16] These kinds of shortages would necessitate a greater reliance on horses.

Infantry divisions in France also had widely varying experiences in obtaining their requisite number of horses. The 276th

Infantry Division, assembling in southern France in early 1944, had no trouble obtaining horses of good quality locally.[17] By contrast, the 7llth Infantry Division, which had been in France since the spring of 1943, still lacked horses for transportation when it left its coastal sector for the front in Normandy.[18] This becomes all the more striking when one considers that the division's artillery, the component that required the most horses for transport, consisted of captured French pieces that had been placed in fixed fortifications along the coast and thus were left behind.[19]

In other divisions the problem was equipment. The 352nd Infantry Division, soon to play an important part in the defense of Omaha Beach, though organized as early as December 1943, could not begin its artillery training until February 1944, because the sights for the guns and harnesses for the horses had not arrived.[20] The 272nd Infantry Division, assembled at about the same time as the 352nd, was experiencing similar problems.[21]

A much more thorny problem was fodder. By the spring of 1944, the German Army in the west consisted of some fifty-eight divisions, of which ten were mobile.[22] The rest, of course, were infantry divisions that relied largely on horses for transport. In terms of men and horses, by 1 March 1944 total German strength in the area of OB West was 1,644,644 men and 114,921 horses. Of these, some 865,179 men and 103,475 horses were controlled by the army. The Luftwaffe had 326,000 men under its command, and also some 4,139 horses. The army's strength was divided as follows: the Seventh Army had 197,946 men and 33,739 horses, while the Fifteenth Army, with most of the panzer divisions positioned in its area, had 312,604 men and 33,162 horses.[23]

Since many of the infantry divisions were located in fixed positions along the coast, fodder could not be collected locally but rather had to be shipped to the units by rail. Here the German Army encountered its first problem with what was to become its nemesis in the west—Allied air power. By early 1944, although the Luftwaffe still retained some degree of control of Germany's skies (especially at night), those of western Europe were dominated by the qualitatively and quantitatively superior Allied air forces.[24] During the spring of 1944 the Allied air forces embarked on a campaign to disrupt the rail network and road system in France. Throughout April and May 1944, air raids were launched against rail yards, bridges, and junctions. Although German repair efforts were considerable, by D-Day most of the bridges over the Seine River had been knocked out.[25]

This aerial offensive created problems for German infantry divisions dependent on the rail system for their supply of fodder. The effectiveness of the transportation plan can be gauged from the fact that almost a full month before the invasion, the Seventh Army was complaining to Army Group B that Allied interdiction of the rail system was creating fodder shortages for units in Brittany. If this situation persisted, local peasant farms would have to be looted for fodder.[26]

The ever-present specter of air power raised another concern for the German commanders, one which had important consequences. This concerned the strategy being developed by the German commanders to meet the expected invasion. The commander of OB West, von Rundstedt, wanted to keep the panzer divisions back near Paris as a reserve. Thus, they would be positioned to intervene decisively en masse against any Allied incursion.[27]

Von Rundstedt's theoretical subordinate, Rommel, who commanded Army Group B, saw things differently.[28] Based on his experience in North Africa, Rommel believed that Allied air power would drastically curtail the ability of the Germans to make long distance strategic moves. He felt that von Rundstedt and von Schweppenburg, the commander of Panzer Group West, underestimated the effects of Allied air power, as their combat service had been on the eastern front, where the effects of air power were diffused over a front extending thousands of miles. Experiences of German troops in Italy seemed to bear out Rommel's worries. During the retreat north from the Gustav Line in May and June 1944, the Fourteenth Army reported high losses in both horses and vehicles from air attack, fighter-bombers being especially dangerous.[29] Given these circumstances, Rommel wanted the panzers located as near to the coast as possible. If the invasion was to be stopped, it had to be held at the water's edge.[30]

Ultimately, the dispute was resolved by Hitler, who decided, predictably, on a compromise. Three panzer divisions, the 2nd, 21st, and 116th, were placed under Rommel's tactical command, but their deployment areas were determined by OKW.[31] Three more divisions, the 9th, 11th, and 2nd SS (*Das Reich*) Panzer Divisions, were assigned to Colonel General Johannes Blaskowitz's Army Group G, and the remaining four, the powerful Panzer Lehr, 17th SS (*Götz von Berlichingen*) Panzer Grenadier, and 1st SS (*Leibstandarte Adolf Hitler*) and 12th SS (*Hitler Jugend*) Panzer Divisions were placed under the direct command of OKW, that is, Hitler.[32] In addition, Hitler made the release of OKW's panzer divisions dependent upon his permission.[33] Thus, even before the onset of the invasion, the Germans were handicapped by a strategy based on compromise, and this played no small part in the German defense ultimately falling between two stools.

Most of the deliberations outlined on the preceding pages concerned the employment of the panzer divisions. Indeed, historically it has come down to us as the Rommel-von Rundstedt "panzer controversy," as one recent article put it.[34] But what of the infantry? If the German defense was to be successful, the infantry divisions would have to hold major portions of the line, thus granting the panzers the freedom of action they required in order to act offensively. This would involve, however, having a number of infantry divisions from other areas of northwestern Europe travel over fairly long distances to the front. These divisions could move part of the way by rail, but then would have to march overland. The overland moves could only be made, however, during the short summer nights. Any attempt to move over the roads in daylight would make a very inviting target for the ubiquitous Allied fighter-bombers.

Matters were made worse now that German infantry divisions were more dependent on horses than ever.

In 1939, a first wave infantry division was manned by 17,734 officers and men. For support it relied on 48 artillery pieces (12 150mm and 36 105mm guns). The division's transport was provided by some 615 trucks and 919 horse-drawn vehicles, of which 196 were allocated to each of the three infantry regiments (a total of 588), while 240 were assigned to the divisional artillery. The division required 4,842 horses.[35] By 1944, however, this establishment could no longer be maintained. The 1944 division (theoretically at least) had an authorized strength of 12,772 officers and men. Its artillery had been reduced to 30 105mm and 9 150mm guns. The number of trucks was cut back from 615 to 370, a 40 percent reduction. Although the number of horses was reduced to 3,177, the number of horse-drawn vehicles was increased by over 30 percent to 1,375.[36] It is important to bear in mind that the standard German horse-drawn vehicle, after being hitched up to a team of horses, took up more space than a truck. Thus, the rear elements of a 1944 German infantry division probably took up more road space than before. Thus, should the Allies be able to turn the invasion into a war of movement, the slow-moving German infantry divisions would be an easy target for the combination of Allied fighter-bombers and the fully motorized Allied ground forces. This may have been partly the reason behind Rommel's statement considering a mobile campaign a poor alternative to a more static defense, even though many other German commanders were "crazy" for mobile warfare.[37]

The infantry divisions were hard hit right from the beginning. The 352nd Infantry Division, defending Omaha Beach, reported that in the first eight days of the invasion, it lost 200 horses killed and reported a further 950 horses missing, although 74 of those were later recovered.[38] The 716th Infantry Division, covering the three British beaches, suffered some 1,138 horse casualties before the end of June, and that was based only on incomplete information.[39] Immediate replace-

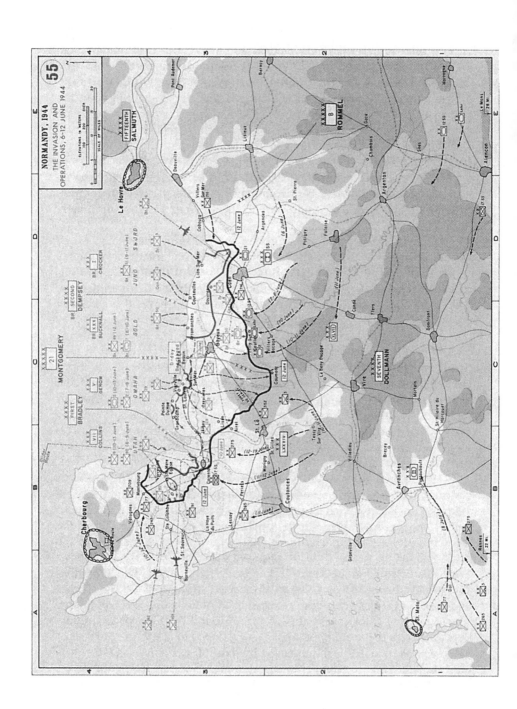

NORMANDY, 1944
THE INVASION AND
OPERATIONS, 6-12 JUNE 1944

ments were obtained locally. Even the panzer divisions took part in this. The I SS Panzer Corps reported that the 21st Panzer Division seized some 210 horses and turned them over to the hard-pressed LXXXVI Corps.[40]

For the infantry divisions that had to travel to the front from other areas of France and Belgium, experiences varied widely. The 276th Infantry Division had problems moving its artillery to Normandy because German equipment once again proved too heavy and also the division's horses had not been broken in properly. In addition, the pattern of sleeping by day and moving by night eventually proved physically debilitating to both men and horses.[41] The 85th Infantry Division, which moved to Normandy from Abbeville in early August, was able to accomplish its march without difficulty. Although harassed by air attacks as it moved overland, the division was able to make use of a series of small depots that had been set up along the unit's line of march (under whose authority is not clear). At these depots the division was able to exchange worn-out horses for fresh animals and to obtain fodder for them.[42] By contrast, the journey of *Kampfgruppe Heintz* from Brittany to the front just after D-Day was a nightmare. Composed of elements of the 275th Infantry Division, it was ordered to Normandy on the morning of 6 June. Normally, the trip should have taken about two days by rail, the distance being only about 120 miles. Constant Allied air attacks, however, turned the trip into an ordeal that lasted about a week.[43]

As expected, movements over long distances could be made only at night. This was particularly hard on the infantry divisions. Because of the widespread disruption of the rail system, the infantry divisions had to move mostly on foot. These marches, plus the alteration of normal sleeping patterns, served to exhaust both men and horses. This cost the Germans a great deal of valuable time. Additional time was also lost because horses killed or disabled by air attacks had to be replaced.[44]

Tactically, the Seventh Army was not severely hindered by its reliance on horses. Horse hospitals had been sited before the invasion in areas relatively inaccessible to air attack, so heavy losses could be avoided. The Seventh Army's veterinary officer, General Doctor Paul Leitner, also reported that grazing areas were abundantly available.[45] The weather was generally warm and sunny. While this helped make Allied fighter-bombers a constant threat, the conditions were helpful for the general health of the horses. At no time did disease ever appear a problem. Even after almost a month of combat operations, Army Group B reported no serious veterinary problems.[46] Most important, however, was that throughout June and for most of July the battlefield remained relatively static. The Germans could even make occasional tactical moves with their horse-drawn elements. Just before the battle of St. Lo, which marked the onset of Operation Cobra, for example, the 352nd Infantry Division was able to regroup and redeploy its artillery.[47]

The drawbacks to the German Army's reliance on horse-drawn transport only became fully apparent in the aftermath of the breakout following Cobra, which began on 24 July. Once the front had been broken and Hitler's attempt to restore it with the Mortain counterattack had foundered on 9 August, the Germans had to retreat as best they could. The retreat was a nightmare, as Allied fighter-bombers swarmed all over the retreating German columns. Owing to the pell-mell nature of the German retreat, motorized units became intermingled with horse-drawn units. Columns were often blocked by disabled horses. In retreating across the Orne River in August, the 353rd Infantry Division found its road blocked several times by damaged vehicles and dead horses.[48] Here was another crucial difference between horses and motor vehicles. Vehicles might still be able to function if slightly damaged. If a horse was killed or disabled, then the horse-drawn vehicle was lost as well. Matters were made worse by the fact that the horse-drawn transport was road-bound, thus making it even more vulnerable to Allied tactical air power. In the 353rd Infantry Division's case, this was especially true in the area east of the Orne, which was open and devoid of the cover the bocage country of Normandy provided to some degree.[49]

Aside from having to cope with Allied air power, the Germans now had to worry about Allied motor power. As noted previously, the Allied ground forces were completely motorized. While not a factor during the relatively static period of the campaign, things became quite different once the campaign assumed a more mobile character. The fully motorized Allied units were able to move much faster than the fuel-starved and horse-dependent German forces. This contributed in no small part to General George Patton's Third Army getting around the German left flank after the Mortain counterattack and ultimately forming the Falaise pocket.

Harassed by constant air attack and artillery bombardment, the Germans not surprisingly suffered enormous losses in horse-drawn vehicles, guns, horses, and veterinary personnel. The 275th Infantry Division's horse-drawn transport and veterinary company were totally lost during the retreat.[50] The 346th Infantry Division lost its artillery, consisting of captured French pieces, and much of its transportation in late August because it lacked the bridging equipment to get the vehicles across the Seine River, about six hundred yards wide at the division's crossing point.[51] In fact, some infantry divisions were actually able to motorize themselves in the course of the retreat, as their surviving trucks proved sufficient to fulfill the transport needs of the shattered and much-shrunken infantry divisions.[52]

Hitler's hopes of reversing the tide of war by halting the Allied invasion had been thoroughly smashed. Losses had been enormous. From 6 June to 1 September, total German casualties were 400,000 men, including 45,000 captured in the Falaise pocket.[53] Although the number of horses lost is impossible to determine precisely, a reasonable estimate may be made from the following data. On 1 June 1944 the Seventh Army reported a ration strength of 311,200 men and 43,000 horses. By 20 June this had risen to 450,000 men and 48,000 horses. The last ten days of June, however, showed a decline to 420,000 men and 45,000 horses.[54] By 15 July casualties had mounted to 97,000 men, with replacements lacking.[55] In equipment, between 6 June and 1 September, the German Army lost

1,800 tanks and assault guns, 1,500 other guns, and 20,000 vehicles of all kinds.[56] In the Falaise pocket alone an incomplete counting of the booty included 2,000 wagons, 700 towed guns, and the corpses of 1,800 horses.[57] From these figures, and given the transport losses suffered by the infantry divisions, the total number of horses lost may be deduced as running over 30,000.

The summer brought equally bad news for German arms on the eastern front. Instead of the Ukraine being the focus of the action, as it had been the two previous years, Soviet attention was now shifted to the front held by Army Group Center, which bulged eastward from the northern edge of the Pripet Marsh. To accomplish the goal of destroying Army Group Center, Stalin and STAVKA assembled a massive number of men supported by huge amounts of equipment under the first, second, and third Byelorussian fronts, as well as the first Baltic front. By 22 June 1944, the four fronts had gathered some 1,254,000 men, 24,000 guns and mortars, 2,306 rocket launchers, 2,715 tanks, 1,355 self-propelled guns, and 70,000 trucks, supported by 5,327 aircraft.[58] The Soviets had a superiority of better than ten to one in tanks and seven to one in aircraft.[59]

For the German Army in the east confronting the burgeoning power of the Soviet Army, air power was seldom a problem, although a horse-drawn vehicle was an inviting target for a fighter or ground-attack aircraft. Although the Soviets enjoyed general air superiority, its effects were somewhat mitigated by the length of the front, which tended to diffuse the striking power of air forces. Nonetheless, the Fourth Army noted that a new feature during the winter battles of 1943/44 was the use of heavy air strikes against German artillery positions in preparation for an offensive. The prescribed antidote was to strengthen the antiaircraft defenses for the artillery.[60] Generally, however, air power in the east was not the problem that it was in the west. Rather, the problem was one of motorized mobility versus horse-drawn mobility.

Although the Soviet Army still employed large numbers of horses, by 1944 it was both mechanized and motorized to a far greater degree than the German Army. While Soviet industry provided just about all of the Soviet Army's tanks, tank destroyers, and artillery pieces, lend-lease aid from Britain and the United States was vital in providing the Soviet Army the soft-skinned transport needed for strategic mobility. Through lend-lease, the Allies sent 427,000 motor vehicles, mostly trucks, to the Soviet Union. These represented almost two-thirds of the total number of motor vehicles held by the Soviet Army at the end of the war.[61] German truck production, by way of comparison, hit a high in 1943 of 109,000, of which a little over half went to the army. Losses in trucks incurred from January to August 1944 alone equaled this figure.[62] To make matters worse, even at this late date, many trucks used by the German Army were really vehicles designed for commercial use and unsuited to military operations.[63]

Aside from the handicap of numerical inferiority, Army Group Center was comparatively immobile. By 22 June 1944, of the German Army's mobile element twelve panzer and panzer grenadier divisions were in France, either fighting in Normandy or awaiting a second amphibious invasion. Several were in Italy, retreating north from Rome toward the Gothic Line. On the eastern front, there were about twenty-four panzer and panzer grenadier divisions. Of these, some eighteen were in the area of Army Groups North and South Ukraine.[64] This deployment happened because both Hitler and OKH expected the Soviet summer offensive to occur in that area. This left Army Group Center very short of mobile units. In all of Army Group Center (Second, Fourth, Ninth, and Third Panzer Armies), there were only five panzer and panzer grenadier divisions.[65] These divisions were below strength and limited in mobility owing to fuel shortages.[66] Although most infantry divisions were in reasonably decent shape, they were dependent on horses for mobility. Again, precise numbers for Army Group Center as a whole are impossible to obtain, but some reasonable deductions can be made from the available data. The Second Army, for which precise information is available, was the smallest of Army Group Center's armies. By 20 June 1944 it had some 56,073 horses. If one includes the Hungarian II Corps, the total increased to 69,297 horses.[67] If we assume that an infantry division averaged between 4,000 and 5,000 horses, and compare that to the percentage of mobility for each division in the Fourth, Ninth, and Third Panzer Armies as given in Rolf Hinze's work, *Der Zusammenbruch der Heeresgruppe Mitte im Osten 1944*, a reasonable estimate, I believe, can be arrived at. Using this criteria, Army Group Center had anywhere from 160,000 to 200,000 horses.[68]

The offensive, timed to coincide with the third anniversary of Operation Barbarossa, opened on 22 June 1944. Progress was immediate and rapid. Although a timely retreat might have mitigated the disaster somewhat, Hitler clung to his delusory fortress policy, introduced on 8 March 1944 in Führer Order 11, which mandated no retreats.[69] When Soviet advances compelled German units to retreat west in attempts to avoid encirclement and annihilation, they could not move rapidly enough to escape the faster-moving Soviet units.[70] For the Germans, even moving trucks around was difficult. Allied air attacks on German oil sources had created severe fuel shortages, which demanded the strictest fuel economy. In addition, the Second Army reported that most of its vehicles were old and worn out, with no replacements available. The Second Army, even with all its horses, was still short of draft horses.[71]

The end result was a disaster of almost unimaginable proportions. Of Army Group Center's thirty-eight divisions, some twenty-five had been destroyed, most of them infantry.[72] Again, it is impossible to determine precisely how many horses were lost in the catastrophe. Some idea may be gained by looking at the fate of one particular infantry division. The 260th Infantry Division, part of the VI Army Corps, had been slightly reinforced by two battalions from the 57th Infantry Division before the Soviet offensive and was about 75 percent mobile.[73] Given the criteria outlined previously for determining the number of horses per division, we can estimate that the 260th had somewhere between 3,000 and 4,000 horses. As the offensive developed, the 260th was committed with four other divisions to the holding of "fortress" Vitebsk. After being surrounded, a breakout was ordered, but most of the garrison was lost. When the remnants of the division were reassembled on 12 August, the 260th had been reduced to 32 officers, 17 clerks, 257 NCOs, 890 men, and 118 Soviet auxiliary personnel or "Hiwis." Its equipment included 3 motorcycles, 2 cars, 35 trucks, 2 light infantry guns, 93 horse-drawn vehicles, and 312 horses.[74] Given the number of infantry divisions destroyed, even if we estimate the number of horses lost per division at just 2,000, Army Group Center lost at least 70,000 to 80,000 horses along with 350,000 men.[75] By the time Model was able to patch the front back together by August, the Germans had been thrown all the way back to the Vistula River. German rule in Russia was at an end.

After the Falaise disaster and the retreat across France, the Germans were finally able to halt the Allied advance near the German border. By careful husbanding of equipment and manpower, Hitler was actually able to create an armored reserve of rebuilt panzer and panzer grenadier divisions. This force of twelve mobile divisions would be supported by some eighteen infantry divisions (now called Volksgrenadier) divisions.[76] Under the command of the Fifth and Sixth Panzer Armies, this force would assault the thinly held American lines in the Ardennes, the scene of Hitler's great victory in 1940. Once through, the panzers would cross the Meuse and head northwest to Antwerp, cutting off the British Twenty-First Army Group. The attack was initially set by Hitler for 25 November, but events on other sectors of the front forced its postponement until mid-December.[77]

How many horses were involved in the attack? Once again, exact numbers do not seem to be available, but a reasonable estimate may be made. According to a fairly reliable work, by January 1945 a German infantry division had an authorized horse strength of 3,057.[78] If multiplied by the number of infantry divisions involved in the attack (eighteen), then the minimum number of horses deployed would have been 55,026. This would be a low estimate, as no account has been taken of corps- and army-level assets, which required horses for mobility.

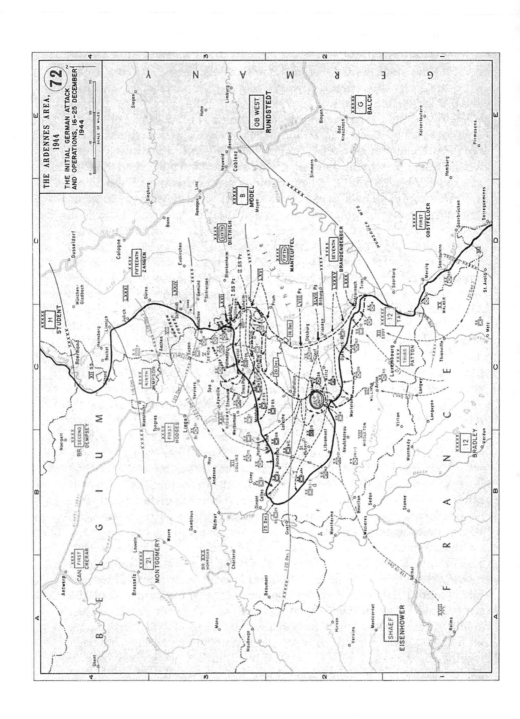

THE ARDENNES AREA, 1944

THE INITIAL GERMAN ATTACK
AND OPERATIONS, 16–25 DECEMBER
1944

SCALE OF MILES

The execution of the attack, however, presented problems. The Ardennes was thickly forested, with narrow, winding roads. This presented a problem in traffic control. Unlike 1940, when the roads were relatively clear and the drive to the Meuse not heavily contested, the German forces would have to effect a breakthrough and then advance against resistance. The question for the Germans in the initial assault was, as in Barbarossa, who should go in first, the infantry or the panzers? Hitler had planned to have the infantry make the initial assault to punch the holes in the line, and then send the panzer divisions through the gaps. Both army commanders, the Sixth Panzer's SS General Josef "Sepp" Dietrich and the Fifth Panzer's General Baron Hasso von Manteuffel, raised objections to this arrangement. Both feared that, given the paucity of roads, the panzers would be blocked in their advance by the horse-drawn transport of the infantry divisions in front of them. Von Manteuffel was able to get this slightly altered after a personal conference with Hitler.[79] Dietrich, although an old crony of the Führer's, chose not to complain directly to Hitler.[80] Rather curiously, he instead raised his qualms about the tactical plan with his immediate superior, Model, who commanded Army Group B and who overruled Dietrich.[81]

The offensive ran into problems right from the start. The Sixth Panzer Army, which was to carry out the offensive's major thrust, ran into the exact situation Dietrich had feared. The Sixth Panzer Army's infantry divisions failed to effect an immediate breakthrough, thus delaying Dietrich's main striking force, a powerful battle group from the 1st SS Panzer Division (*Leibstandarte Adolf Hitler*) under Colonel Joachim Peiper, in the start of his advance. Even when a gap was finally created, Peiper found his planned route of advance blocked by the horse-drawn transport of the 12th Infantry Division, thus forcing Peiper to make a rather lengthy detour.[82] Thus the two most important elements of the operation, time and speed, were lost in the Sixth Panzer Army's sector right at the outset.

Things were not much better in the Fifth Panzer Army's sector, even though von Manteuffel had been able to insert his panzer divisions in the front line.[83] Although this arrangement had allowed von Manteuffel to enjoy greater progress than Dietrich, it also meant that in some cases panzer divisions had to share the same stretches of road simultaneously with infantry divisions. The Panzer Lehr Division, for example, had to share a road with the 26th Infantry Division.[84] The result was that tracked and wheeled motor vehicles, not to mention tanks, became entangled with horse-drawn vehicles. The armored vehicles would often push the horse-drawn vehicles to the side of the road and thus add to the developing traffic jam. What made this even more critical was that the horse-drawn vehicles were carrying ammunition for the infantry.[85] Even when the horse-drawn vehicles got moving again, they had to pass over muddy secondary and dirt roads that had already been badly chewed up by tracked vehicles.[86] Matters were also made worse by the Panzer Lehr, which, despite its élite reputation, showed very poor march discipline on this occasion.[87]

The infantry divisions encountered further problems as the advance proceeded. Fodder was difficult to bring up over the regular supply routes, as gasoline and ammunition had unquestioned priority. Fodder was also difficult if not impossible to obtain from the countryside in winter.[88] Replacements were also becoming hard to come by. Given the heavy losses of horses over the previous years, and the desperate nature of the situation, the German Army resorted to some good old-fashioned looting. The Fifteenth Army, for example, which was to launch an attack against the British in Holland in support of the main offensive, told its units that they could appropriate any horses fit for service, as long as they were located in areas outside of Germany proper.[89]

The defeat of the Ardennes offensive marked the effective end of large-scale operations by the Wehrmacht. Hitler launched an offensive in Hungary in March 1945 to protect his remaining source of oil but used the SS panzer divisions that had only just been transferred from the west. These formations had not recovered from the losses sustained in the Ardennes. Consequently, the offensive enjoyed only a few days of success before being stopped by the Soviets. A similar operation against the Soviets just east of the Oder River in February had been equally ineffective. By that time, however, Hitler had already, in von Manteuffel's words, "started a corporal's war. There were no big plans—only a multitude of piecemeal fights."[90]

Despite these last-ditch offensives, the Allied forces closed in on Germany. In the east the Soviet winter offensive, commencing 12 January 1945, carried the Soviets from the Vistula to the Oder, from which they would launch the final offensive in April to take Berlin. In the west the Allies were able to gain several bridgeheads over the Rhine, the most important being the Remagen Bridge, captured on 7 March. Further Allied operations brought about the encirclement of Army Group B, whose commander, Model, disbanded it before committing suicide on 21 April. On 18 April the Allied offensive began anew in Italy, where German resistance collapsed completely.

With the enormous losses in vehicles suffered in the disasters of 1944 and the loss of Germany's remaining major sources of oil, the German Army undertook one last reorganization of its panzer divisions. The 1945 division would have one of its two tank battalions replaced by a battalion of mechanized infantry. The two infantry regiments were stripped of their motor transport. The division's transportation was augmented by horses serviced by a veterinary platoon. The division would have 11,422 men and 62 tanks.[91] Although no precise figures seem to be available, a reasonably good guess would be that the division employed roughly one thousand horses or more. It is interesting to note that—officially at least—this new organization applied only to army units. Although the SS divisions, reduced by two infantry battalions, were also reorganized slightly, the SS panzer division was still supposed to be completely motorized.[92] Given the general shortages of vehicles, fuel, and drivers, however, it is more than likely that the SS divisions had to employ horses as well. In addition, the other services also had to utilize horses instead of vehicles. In fact, by 1 February 1945 the Wehrmacht deployed some 1,198,724 horses, of which the army had 1,060,106, the Luftwaffe 37,072, and the navy 1,556.[93] Thus, by the end of the war, even the most modern, mechanized elements of the German armed forces ran on oats as much as on gasoline.

CHAPTER 8

Perpetuation of a Myth

A mechanized juggernaut.

The Battle of Russia[1]

You know how I'm sure they're finished out there? The carts. They're using carts to move their wounded and their supplies.

Actor George C. Scott as General George Patton[2]

That a once-mighty German army was reduced to such dependence on horses came as a shock to many who viewed the pitiable debris of the battlefield.

Charles B. MacDonald[3]

We found ourselves driving [in the Po valley)] through fields of passively grazing horses. It was astonishing.

Sir Michael Howard[4]

If the preceding chapters have demonstrated anything, it is that the German Army's lifeblood was oats as much as it was oil. Yet, the popular image of the German Army remains that of a modern, mechanized force. I have presented several lectures and talks on various aspects of the subject under consideration. The normal reaction of the audience is generally one of absolute surprise, and even amazement. Even people who knew better were surprised. Sir Michael Howard, as Battalion Adjutant of the 3rd Battalion, Coldstream Guards, had taken an intelligence course on the German Army and thus was as well informed as anyone as to the true nature of the German Army. Yet even he was amazed at how dependent the Germans actually were on horses. Thus, the myth of the mechanized

119

juggernaut persists. Why? How did this misperception come about?

In attempting to answer these questions, some mention must be made of sources. In this chapter, much of the source material is of a nontextual nature, mainly, newsreel film, documentaries, and even movies. Also, many of the conclusions put forth in this chapter can only be of an intuitive nature, for reasons that will become clear later.

The 1930s and 1940s marked the beginning of the nonprint media age. The 1930s was the great age of radio. Radios were now available in large quantities. Hitler, through the efforts of his later minister of propaganda, Dr. Josef Goebbels, became one of the first politicians to make effective use of this new means of communication.[5]

During the late 1930s and 1940s, the motion picture came into its own as a popular form of entertainment. As part of the show (usually a double feature, at least in the United States), a newsreel was shown. For Goebbels newsreels (*Wochenschau*) represented a potentially powerful means of propaganda, and his ministry closely supervised their production. Goebbels considered them important enough to screen each new *Wochenschau* twice before authorizing its release to movie theaters.[6]

With the beginnings of rearmament, Goebbels applied his talents to presenting the German Army in a specific image. Here, what follows must be of a speculative nature, as there seems to be no documentary "smoking gun." A survey of the catalog dealing with the documents from Goebbels's ministry available on microfilm at the National Archives in Washington, D.C., produced disappointing results. The documents there are mainly concerned with administrative matters, such as the budget, personnel, and other unilluminating bureaucratic minutiae. Nor does Goebbels himself say anything about how the Wehrmacht is presented in his diaries. Nonetheless, from looking at the *Wochenschauen*, one can see that the more mechanized side of the German Army is clearly emphasized.

This was probably for two reasons: First, Goebbels obviously wanted to impress the German people with the modernity, speed, and power of the German Army. This became especially important after the outbreak of the war, which was not greeted with enthusiasm by the German population.[7] The second reason has to do with German foreign policy. The Wochenschauen were circulated abroad quite widely. Even as late as 1944 they were shown in 2,540 theaters outside of Germany.[8] This is important to remember, because for Hitler the German Army, certainly during the late 1930s and the early years of the war, represented not only an instrument of military conquest, but also a means of political intimidation. Although, as stated previously, there seems to be no absolute documentary proof, the emphasizing of the modern elements of the German military would be perfectly consistent with the goal of political intimidation. After all, tanks and dive bombers are a good deal more intimidating than a column of horse-drawn artillery paralyzed by an outbreak of equine pneumonia.

The German propaganda newsreel was all the more effective because of the great effort that went to the collection of combat footage. The Wehrmacht, working hand-in-hand with Goebbels, created propaganda companies (PK). The PK men were trained soldiers who wore regular military uniforms. In civilian life, however, they had worked with filming equipment, and they applied their talents for the army, providing large quantities of high-quality real combat footage.[9]

While Goebbels used films to impress and intimidate, American film maker Frank Capra used the same films for a different reason. During World War II, Capra produced a series of seven films under the general title, *Why We Fight*. The purpose of these films was to educate the American public as to why the United States was fighting in World War II.

Capra, who was greatly impressed with German propaganda films, realized that he could never duplicate them. Instead, he hit on the clever idea of turning Goebbels's own product against the Nazis. Thus, the Why We Fight films use actual footage from the *Wochenschauen* and other German propaganda films.

The Capra films present the same image of the German Army as the Wochenschauen do. If one watches films from the series such as *The Nazis Strike* and *The Battle of Russia*, one notices that an overwhelming percentage of the military footage shows tanks, planes, and motorized equipment. Horses are shown only in ceremonial occasions, such as parades, or in quick "cutaway" shots. These images are reinforced by the narration, which is delivered in a suitably grim and determined tone. The term "mechanized juggernaut" is one that frequently pops up during these films. Although Capra never explicitly states it, the emphasizing of the more modern elements of the German armed forces was perfectly consistent with the ultimate purpose of these films. The *Why We Fight* series was designed to scare people, in order to motivate them to action. In other words, Capra sought to convince people that the Nazis were dangerous, and, as previously stated, tanks, aircraft, and truck-towed 88s look far more dangerous than a column of horse-drawn transportation.

Although they are supposed to be enlightening, documentaries have contributed to the myth. Documentaries do this in both voluntary and involuntary ways. The makers of documentaries are forced to rely on the same film footage discussed before. Thus, in that sense, documentaries involuntarily perpetuate the myth of the mechanized German Army. On the other hand, documentaries do engage at times in blatant distortion of the facts. The best example of this is the acclaimed series produced by the British Broadcasting Corporation (BBC), *The World at War*. The third installment, which deals with the fall of France in 1940, made great mention of the fact that the French Army after World War I placed great reliance on the horse for mobility and transport. It completely overlooked the fact that the German Army, which in 1940 was almost at the peak of its power, was every bit as dependent on the horse for mobility and transport as was the French Army.

Films have also made their contribution to the misperception of the nature of the German Army. Films made during or just after the war did this by depicting the enemy in a rather stereotypical fashion. For varied reasons, including racism, the Japanese were typically depicted as brutal and savage, almost subhuman. The Japanese were presented as being something on the evolutionary scale as somewhere between apes and humans, and closer to apes at that.[10] The Italians were generally depicted in one of three ways: They could be amiable, as is the Italian soldier in *Sahara*. They also could be bumbling and pleasant, as typified by Fortunio Bonanova's portrayal of the Italian general in *Five Graves to Cairo*. Finally they could be irrelevant, as are the Italians depicted in *Casablanca*.

The Germans are also depicted in several ways, and these contribute to the myth. Germans were usually presented as cruel, as exemplified by Erich von Stroheim's performance as the cruel Nazi doctor in *North Star*. They could be ruthless, as typified by Conrad Veidt's performance as the pitiless Major Strasser in *Casablanca*. Finally, Germans could be efficient, with von Stroheim once again providing the model as Rommel in *Five Graves to Cairo*. These portrayals also reinforce the notion of mechanization, as a high degree of motorization would seem to be consonant with the traits of ruthlessness and efficiency. It would be hard to depict people as cruel and ruthless while having them give horses the large amounts of tender loving care they require. It is also important to note that a large number of World War II films were set in North Africa, as most films about World War II were actually made during the war. The importance of the North African setting is also something about which further comment will be made later.

The postwar films, including the big budget epics, did little if anything to correct the false image of the German Army. Part of this comes from the dominance of the North African campaign. It was far and away the most popular setting for war films about the European theater, and certainly no German commander has been portrayed by actors more often than Rommel.[11] Yet, even films that should show horses do not. In Darryl F. Zanuck's *The Longest Day*, perhaps the best film ever made about World War II, there is only one horse belonging to the German Army. Even when the matter of horses is mentioned, the context is incorrect. The best example of this is the film *Patton*. While surveying the carnage after a hard-fought action near the German border, Patton, portrayed by George

C. Scott, proclaims that the Germans are finished because they are now reduced to using horses for transport. Thus, the uninformed viewer gets the impression that the German Army used horses for transport only late in the war and only as a drastic measure, and not as a matter of course right from the start.

As mentioned previously, the North African campaign has played an important part in the creation of the myth of the mechanized German Army, at least in the West. The longest period of time Allied troops (British or American) were in constant contact with German forces was in North Africa, where the campaign lasted (if one excludes the defeat of the first Italian offensive in 1940) for roughly two and one-half years. The campaign certainly captured the popular imagination, as it was replete with swift thrusts, desperate parries, and headlong advances, not to mention popular figures, of whom the most notable was Rommel. None of the armies in the North African desert used horses for obvious reasons. Even the Italians, certainly the most poorly equipped of the belligerents, had completely motorized artillery (meaning guns towed by trucks) and supply transport columns, although it should be pointed out that the Italian forces in North Africa were usually short of transport.[12] The North African campaign certainly contributed to the notion of the mechanized German Army.

General Douglas MacArthur, in his famous speech to Congress on 20 April 1951, made perhaps his most famous statement when he said: "Old soldiers never die. They just fade away."[13] To be absolutely accurate as to what old soldiers do, he might have added that they write their memoirs. This was certainly true of the German Army. One of the most abundant types of literature dealing with World War II are the memoirs written by scores of high-ranking German officers, including Walter Warlimont, von Manstein, Sigfried Westphal, Guderian, and Friedrich von Mellenthin, to name just a few.

Yet this veritable avalanche of memoirs ultimately contributes little to understanding the true nature of the German Army, primarily because German memoirs can be divided into two basic types, namely, high commanders and field commanders. Memoirs of the higher commanders, the most notable of which is von Manstein's *Lost Victories*, deal mainly with the conduct of operations at a very high level, usually army or army group. In addition, memoirs of this type often deal with the memoirist's relationship with Hitler, often seeking to lay the blame for anything that went wrong at the feet of the long-dead Führer. Even when actual operations are dealt with, the discussion is at such a high level that the matter under discussion in this study is rarely mentioned. One searches *Lost Victories* in vain for any mention of the German Army's dependence on horses and the problems it caused. The same is true for Westphal's *The German Army in the West*. Thus, our picture of the German Army is distorted right from the start.

A number of field commanders at a lower level have written memoirs.

Some of the most popular books include von Senger und Etterlin's *Neither Fear Nor Hope*, Guderian's *Panzer Leader*, and von Mellenthin's *Panzer Battles*. More recently von Luck weighed in with his *Panzer Commander*. The operative word in the majority of these titles is "panzer." All of these officers spent most of their service in the panzer arm. Consequently, the subject of this book is mentioned rarely, if at all. Even the best-known worm's-eye-view memoir of the German Army, Guy Sajer's *The Forgotten Soldier*, deals with someone who spent most of his combat service with the élite *Grossdeutschland* Panzer Division. Thus, memoirs from the field level and lower present a skewed image of the German Army, coming from a branch that comprised only a small portion of the German Army.

Historians also play their part, and have done a poor job in illuminating this aspect of the German Army. The lack of emphasis can be explained largely as a matter of taste. This book, and any other dealing with similar matters, such as transport, is really about logistics. Military historians do not generally deal with logistics for one very good reason—it is *boring*! Most military historians (myself included) prefer the cut and thrust of exciting campaigns, occasionally playing a sort of military Monday morning quarterback. Others prefer to deal with the more colorful personalities or brilliant commanders of war. Rommel and Patton, for example, are favorite subjects of World War II biographers.

Logistics, however, has always taken a back seat. Consider, for example, the American Civil War. It has generated thousands of books and articles. The vast majority of this literature deals mostly with either individual campaigns, battles, or biographies of the leading figures. The number of studies dealing with logistics in the Civil War, however, can be counted on the fingers of one's hands. It is the same with World War II.

Even when authors do deal with logistics, horses receive relatively little attention. The relevant chapters of van Creveld's interesting work, *Supplying War,* for example, deal more with matters relating to the motorized forces. In campaign studies, authors generally give logistical matters short shrift, preferring to deal with them in a page or two.

When authors do deal with the German Army's reliance on horses, they do so in ways that often leave readers with an inaccurate impression. Charles B. MacDonald, for example, as quoted at the beginning of this chapter, gives the impression that the German Army used horses on a large scale only late in the war because of losses suffered earlier.[14] This assertion was made in 1969 and echoed a similar statement made by him in another book in 1963.[15] In fairness to MacDonald, it should be pointed out that more recent historians' works also make the same error. Carlo D'Este, for example, makes the same error in his otherwise brilliant book, *Decision in Normandy,* saying in a note that "it was a measure of the seriousness of the German situation in Normandy that what was once the most modern army in the world was reduced to the use of horsepower."[16]

Thus, even historians have played their part in perpetuating the myth of the mechanized German Army. In this sense, we as historians have failed not only the reading public at large, but our own profession as well.

Conclusion

A horse! a horse! my kingdom for a horse!
William Shakespeare[1]

So spoke Richard III, at least according to Shakespeare. Had Richard been in command of the German Army, he would have had no trouble in having his rather urgent wish fulfilled. In the preceding pages, I have examined how the German Army employed horses and tried to indicate the scale on which they were used. In doing so, I hope that the notion of the German Army as "mechanized juggernaut" has been definitively shattered. What other conclusions, however, can be drawn from this book, especially with regard to the questions posed at the beginning?

In force structure the use of horses had several effects, some intended and some not. The most obvious was the creation of specialized mobile formations, such as the panzer and motorized infantry (later panzer grenadier) divisions and their concentration into corps-sized units.[2] For the Germans this was the obviously correct solution, given the state of German doctrinal thinking regarding the employment of tanks. To have spread tanks and vehicles among the infantry divisions would have been the height of folly, as the infantry divisions still would have had to rely on horses for transport and would have diffused the striking power of the Wehrmacht's best offensive weapon to the point of irrelevance, as the French Army discovered in 1940.

The division of the German Army into two distinct components, one armored and motorized and the other not, could have produced some serious consequences for the performance of the German Army. That it did not was due to the common-sense approach of the German Army toward doctrine and training. Generally, the Inspector-General of Panzer Troops was the final authority on all matters concerning tanks. When Guderian was appointed to the post on 28 February 1943, he made certain that all doctrine and training policies on tanks were binding on the rest of the army.[3] Thus, even though the army's separate parts were quite different, the whole was on the same sheet of music in terms of training with tanks. This allowed the Germans to effectively employ ad hoc units such as *Korpsgruppe Fischer*, composed of elements of the 10th Panzer Division and the 334th Infantry Division, which played an important part in preventing the Allies from completing a rapid occupation of Tunisia in early 1943.[4]

There was another side to this, however. While the infantry was required to learn and understand the limitations of tanks, the opposite was not true. While this did not really affect enlisted men and NCOs, it did affect officers, especially as they rose in rank toward divisional and corps command. Many officers who had spent their careers with the panzer troops now had to command infantry divisions or corps containing infantry divisions, and they failed to grasp the limitations imposed on the divisions by their reliance on horse-drawn transport, often demanding too much of the horses.[5] It is also worth noting that training courses for senior officers included two hours of instruction on horses.[6]

The deleterious effects of the German Army's dependence on horses for transport on its operational performance were not immediately apparent. The Polish and French campaigns were comparatively easy from the standpoint of horses, although some hard fighting was required. The striking power of the panzer arm was maximized by concentration, and the distances to be covered by the infantry divisions were not prohibitive, so that they were able to catch up to the panzers relatively quickly. In addition the weather, generally warm and dry, cooperated beautifully.[7] The Norwegian campaign was not particularly hard on the German Army, although it effectively eliminated the German surface navy as a factor and emasculated Germany's amphibious capability, which was never formidable anyway.

The defects in Germany's army, economy, and approach to war finally became evident during Operation Barbarossa. The inability of the German economy to produce the requisite number of motor vehicles led the German Army to utilize large numbers of foreign vehicles, mainly of French design.[8] These were not really suitable to conditions in the Soviet Union and soon broke down. Even the German vehicles were having problems, since many of them were really commandeered civilian trucks not designed for the wear and tear of military operations.[9]

The 1941 campaign also exposed the inherent flaw in the dual nature of the German Army by introducing the factors of distance and weather. The vast distances in the Soviet Union ultimately proved insurmountable. It accentuated the difference in the marching capabilities between the motorized units and the nonmotorized formations. The part played by the failure to draw the initial encircling nets tight enough and the subsequent escape of large numbers of Soviet troops in the ultimate collapse of Barbarossa should not be underestimated. By an ironic twist of fate, however, once the bad weather set in and the Soviets went over to the offensive in December, horses proved instrumental to the Wehrmacht's survival, as most of the vehicles were inoperative and horse-drawn sleds provided the only certain means of delivering supplies.[10]

The dual nature of the German Army and the shoestring-like nature of the German logistical effort in Russia came to the fore once again in the ill-fated 1942 summer campaign. The panzer armies, now including a larger number of infantry formations, were so slow in their advance that the Soviet forces were generally able to escape encirclement. Once again, the element of space proved impossible to overcome in the inhospitable steppes. The inability of the surrounding area and the overstretched German railway system to provide adequate amounts of fodder led to the effective immobilization of the Sixth Army at Stalingrad by the autumn, when most of the horses were sent to rest areas as far west as behind the Dnepr River.[11] Horse-drawn transport had helped lead the German

Army in 1941 to a near disaster. In 1942, it helped lead the Wehrmacht into an irredeemable catastrophe.

After Stalingrad, the increasing motorization of the Soviet Army gave it a strategic mobility that the Germans could not hope to match. Once the Germans lost the initiative at Kursk, it was never to be regained. The culmination of the simultaneous trends of increasing Soviet as opposed to decreasing German mobility was reached in the catastrophe that befell Army Group Center in late June 1944.

In the west, German forces faced not only the same inferiority in strategic mobility but also overwhelming Allied tactical air power. Once the Allies had secured a firm foothold in Normandy, the collapse of the German defense became a mere matter of time, something the German Army could not prevent but only stave off temporarily, despite its enormous tactical competence. Thus, the reliance on horses for transport clearly had an important impact on German military operations.

Given what we have seen in the preceding pages, do we have to recast our ideas about the nature of World War II in general and the German Army in particular? I think it imperative that, in order to gain a truer perspective of the war, we must alter our conception of the German Army. That the mechanized juggernaut was a myth has, I think, been convincingly demonstrated. How then can the German Army be defined? Perhaps the best way would be to say that it was a more highly perfected version of the force that almost brought victory to General Erich Ludendorf in 1918. In its outlook, operational doctrines, and tactics, the force was closely related to the German Army of World War I. It clearly espoused the notion of the "battle of annihilation" (*Vernichtungsschlacht*), the basis of Alfred von Schlieffen's ideas, which influenced Germany's conduct in both world wars.[12] The German Army's tactics in World War II clearly were based on those developed in the latter stages of World War I.[13] The only major difference was the fitting of tanks and supporting aircraft into the concept. These notable developments aside, the bulk of the German Army that fought World War II was not far removed from

its imperial predecessor of World War I, or even of the nineteenth century.

In broader terms, the German Army's reliance on horses
for transport also suggests a new way of looking at World War
II. It is important to remember that all of the European armies
against whom the Germans enjoyed success, namely Poland,
France, Belgium, Holland, Greece, Yugoslavia, and the Soviet
Union (initially), were essentially mirror images of the major
part of the German Army.[14] As long as these conditions prevailed, the more modern motorized elements of the German
Army, the panzer and motorized infantry divisions concen-
trated into powerful striking forces, could play a decisive role.
The divisions constituted a striking force that some of these
European armies, such as those of Poland and Belgium, could
not match in equipment, while against the French in 1940, the
difference lay in the superiority of German doctrine, training,
and leadership.[15]

All of this changed, however, after December 1941. Once
the Grand Alliance, to use Churchill's phrase, of the Soviet
Union, Britain, and the United States could begin to make its
combined strength felt, Germany's defeat was inevitable.
Churchill's own certainty about this speaks volumes. When
informed of the United States's entry into the war, his initial
comment was "so, we had won after all."[16]

There is another way of looking at this, which is in economic
terms. As stated previously, the German Army did well in the
years of "Blitzkrieg" against armies that similarly depended on
horses for transport. It is also important to remember, however,
why this was so. These other European countries lacked either
the capacity to produce large numbers of motor vehicles, the
requisite amount of oil to fuel them, or both. Those countries,
like Germany, had poor vehicle-to-people ratios. France, for
example, in 1933 had one vehicle for every twenty-five people.
By 1937 this had declined to one vehicle for every nineteen people. Curiously, these figures were slightly superior to those for
England, which had one vehicle for every twenty-nine people in
1933, improving to one vehicle for every twenty-one people by

1937.[17] In France's case, improvement was slow because French industry failed to modernize its plant during the interwar period.[18] Although England's numbers were slightly poorer, its rate of improvement was greater, owing to the almost constant expansion of automobile production during the 1930s.[19] Yet it is important to note that Germany's ratio was far worse, even with improvement, going from one vehicle for every eighty-nine people in 1933 to one for every forty-seven people by 1937, the worst in Europe except for Italy.[20]

In a larger economic sense, these figures indicate, to me at least, that the economics of such countries as France and Germany were not really modern. German industry, for example, still employed techniques and organization more attuned to the nineteenth century. The supply of armaments components, for example, was severely hindered by the fact that they were often manufactured by a large number of small-scale concerns scattered throughout the countryside. Many of these were no more than workshops employing no more than thirty men. Although this provided some protection from the effects of bombing, it also made mass production almost an impossibility.[21] In addition, German industry relied heavily on skilled labor, of which there was a shortage.[22]

Once the early years of the war had passed, Germany found itself confronted by a coalition of the mightiest industrial powers in the world.[23] Although the Soviet Union was lacking an automobile industry, trucks supplied by lend-lease certainly made up for this deficiency. In addition, the Allied powers and neutral countries possessed over 90 percent of the world's oil refining capacity, with the United States and the Soviet Union alone accounting for almost 70 percent. Against this, Germany, Italy, and the occupied territories, plus the minor Axis powers, could account for only a mere 4 percent of the world's refining capacity.[24] Given these circumstances, Germany's situation was clearly hopeless after the miscarriage of Barbarossa.

How then, can we sum up? Perhaps it would be best to say that the German Army, although forward looking in some important ways, was essentially a late World War I army, supported by an economy rooted in many ways in the nineteenth century and fighting for one of the most evil causes of history. When confronted by a coalition of modern economic and military powers firmly committed to Hitler's destruction, there could be little doubt about the final outcome.

Notes

INTRODUCTION

1. Martin van Creveld, *Supplying War* (New York, 1980), 143.
2. As late as 1944, when the number of German Army, SS and Luftwaffe panzer, and panzer grenadier (including parachute) divisions reached a high of forty-eight, they still comprised only about 16 percent of the total number of German divisions or division-size equivalents. Army High Command (OKH), Summary of Large Units of the Army, the Waffen SS, and the Parachute Troops, as of 30 July 1944, 31 July 1944, National Archives Records Section Microfilm Series T-78/Roll 413/Frame 6381074. (Hereafter cited as NARS T-78/413/6381074.)
3. This question has been briefly discussed in R. L. DiNardo and Austin Bay, "Horse-Drawn Transport in the German Army," *Journal of Contemporary History* 23, no. 1 (January 1988): 129–42.
4. Gerd Hardach, *The First World War 1914–1918* (Berkeley, 1981), 112.

CHAPTER 1

1. Quoted in Heinz Guderian, *Panzer Leader* (1952; reprint, Washington, D.C., 1979), 29. The occasion for this statement was the first time armored and motorized units were demonstrated before Hitler.
2. Unsigned, "Das Pferd in Heer und Wirtschaft von heute," *Militär Wochenblatt* 121, no. 41 (23 April 1937): 2538.
3. Holger H. Herwig, "The Dynamics of Necessity: German Military Policy during the First World War," in Allan R. Millett and Williamson Murray, eds., *Military Effectiveness: The First World War*, vol. 1 (Boston, 1988), 93.
4. Guderian, *Panzer Leader*, 19–24.
5. For details see Barton Whaley, *Covert German Rearmament, 1919–1939: Deception and Misperception* (Frederick, Md., 1984), 1–40.
6. Adolf Hitler, *Mein Kampf* (1943; reprint, Boston, 1971), 610.
7. Walter Nehring, *Die Geschichte der deutschen Panzerwaffe 1916 bis 1945* (Berlin, 1969), 74.
8. van Creveld, *Supplying War*, 142.
9. B. H. Liddell-Hart, *History of the Second World War* (New York, 1972), 23.
10. Berenice A. Carroll, *Design for Total War* (The Hague, 1968), 145.
11. Rolf Wagenführ, *Die deutsche Industrie im Kriege 1939–1945* (Berlin, 1955), 55.

12. State Office of Economic Planning, "The Importance of Economic Raw Materials of South Eastern Europe For the Germany Economy," March 1939, NARS T-84/80/ 1367770.

13. Hans-Erich Völkman, "Die NS Wirtschaft unter dem 'Neuen Plan,'" in Militärgeschichtlichen Forschungsamt, *Das Deutsche Reich und der Zweite Weltkrieg*, vol. 1 (Stuttgart, 1979–88), 271.

14. Brian R. Mitchell, *European Historical Statistics 1750–1975*, 2d ed. (New York, 1981), 393–94.

15. Robert Goralski and Russell W. Freeburg, *Oil and War* (New York, 1987), 21.

16. Burton H. Klein, *Germany's Economic Preparations for War* (Cambridge, Mass., 1959), 32.

17. Maurice Williams, "German Imperialism and Austria, 1938," *Journal of Contemporary History* 14, no. 1 (January 1979): 144.

18. Goralski and Freeburg, *Oil and War*, 17–21.

19. U.S. Strategic Bombing Survey, "The Effects of Strategic Bombing on the German War Economy" (Washington, D.C., 31 October 1945): 75. (Hereafter cited as USSBS.)

20. Hans Umbreit, "Die Ausbeutung der besetzen Gebiete," in Militärgeschichtlichen Forschungsamt, *Das Deutsche Reich und der Zweite Weltkrieg*, vol. 5, 212.

21. Carroll, *Design for Total War*, 122.

22. R. J. Overy, *Göring: The "Iron Man"* (London, 1984), 45.

23. International Military Tribunal, *Trial of the Major War Criminals* (Nuremberg, 1947–49), Document PS-3730, vol. 33, 33–37. (Hereafter cited as IMT, TTMWC, Doc. PS-3730, vol. 33, 33–37. All IMT documents will be cited in this form.)

24. IMT, TTMWC, Doc. EC-420, vol. 36, 498–500.

25. Wilhelm Deist, *The Wehrmacht and German Rearmament* (London, 1981), 83.

26. Jost Dülffer, "Determinants of German Naval Policy, 1920–1939, in Wilhelm Deist, ed., *The German Military in the Age of Total War* (Dover, N.H., 1985), 166.

27. Albert Speer, *Inside the Third Reich* (New York, 1970), 250.

28. USSBS, "German Motor Vehicle Industry Report" (Washington, D.C., January 1947), 5.

29. Guderian, "Kraftfahrtruppen," *Militärwissenschaftliche Rundschau* 1, no. 1, (December 1935): 74.

30. Reichs-Kredit-Gesellschaft, *Theibstoffwirtschaft in der Welt und in Deutschland*, c. 1939, NARS T-84/51/1332658.

31. IMT, TTMWC, Doc. PS-2654, vol. 31, 59–63.

32. H. W. Koch, *The Hitler Youth* (New York, 1976), 230.

33. Kenneth Macksey, *Guderian: Panzer General* (London, 1975), 61.

34. Klaus-Jürgen Müller, *General Ludwig Bech* (Boppard-am-Rhein, 1980), 171.

35. Ibid., 209. For a rather mendacious view of Beck as an arch reactionary opposed to motorization and the development of the panzer arm, see Guderian, *Panzer Leader*, 32.

36. Deist, *German Military in Total War*, 38.
37. Walter Görlitz, *History of the German General Staff* (New York, 1953), 301.
38. George Gaylord Simpson, *Horses* (New York, 1951), 44.
39. Center for Military History, Manuscript #P-090, Burkhart Müller-Hillebrand, "Horses in the German Army (1941–1945)," 1952, 18. (Hereafter cited as CMH, MSS #P-090. All CMH manuscripts will be cited in this form.)
40. Ibid., 260.
41. Jock Haswell, *The First Respectable Spy* (London, 1969), 130.
42. George H. Waring, *Horse Behavior* (Park Ridge, Calif., 1983), 76.
43. Ibid., 80.
44. U.S. Department of Agriculture, *Special Report on Diseases of the Horse*, rev. ed. (Washington, D.C., 1942), 448–50.
45. Ibid., 492.
46. CMH, MSS #P-090, 262.
47. Goralski and Freeburg, *Oil and War*, 28.
48. American Military Attaché Report on Remounts for the German Army, 6 December 1934, Military Intelligence Division Report #2672-B-11/1. (Hereafter cited as MID 2672-B-11/1.)
49. CMH, MSS #P-090, 215.
50. German Army, *Pferdeersatzvorschrift*, 30 September 1936, 19. This manual was once available in its original booklet form, but has recently been microfilmed. It is now available in NARS T-78/853. There are no frame numbers on this particular reel.
51. Ibid., 14.
52. CMH, MSS #P-090, 215.
53. Ibid., 218.
54. German Army, *Pferdeersatzvorschrift*, 12.
55. Ibid., 11.
56. Ibid., 12.
57. Ibid., 24.
58. Regulations for Wehrkreis Remount Schools, 22 May 1935, NARS T-79/75/000379.
59. Ibid.
60. German Army, *Pferdeersatzvorschrift*, 13.
61. CMH, MSS #D-098, Maximilian Betzer, "Horse Diseases during the Eastern Campaign (1941–1945)." n.d., 4.
62. CMH, MSS #P-090, 64.
63. Burkhart Müller-Hillebrand, *German Tank Maintenance in World War II* (Washington, D.C., 1954), 41–42.
64. CMH, MSS #P-090, 90.
65. Erich von Manstein, *Aus einem Soldatenleben 1887–1939* (Bonn, 1958), 241.
66. van Creveld, *Supplying War*, 145.
67. Hans Wagner, "Gedanken uber Kampfwagenabwehr," *Militär Wochenblatt* 113, no. 1, (4 July 1928), 10.
68. American Military Attaché Report on German Anti-Tank Units and Tactics, 15 October 1935, MID 2016-1236/1.

69. Martin van Creveld, *Fighting Power* (Westport, Conn., 1982), 62.
70. Eurollydon [pseud.] "The Psychology of the German Regimental Officer," *Royal United Service Institution Journal* 82, no. 528 (November 1937), 777.
71. Williamson Murray, *The Change in the European Balance of Power 1938–1939* (Princeton, 1984), 147–148.
72. After-action Report of the XIII Army Corps on the Occupation of Austria, March-April 1938, 6 May 1938, NARS T-314/525/000319.
73. Vojtech Mastny, *The Czechs under Nazi Rule* (New York, 1971), 66.
74. CMH, MSS #P-103, Hellmuth Reinhardt, "Utilization of Captured Material by Germany in World War II," 1953, 36–37.
75. After-action Report of the XIII Army Corps on the Occupation of Czechoslovakia, September-October 1938, 15 October 1938, NARS T-314/525/000537.
76. Instructions for the Disposition of Czech Equipment, 28 March 1939, NARS T-79/95/000988.
77. Burkhart Müller-Hillebrand, *Das Heer 1933–1945*, vol. 1 (Darmstadt, 1954–1969), 55.

CHAPTER 2

1. Franz Halder, *The Halder Diaries*, vol. 3 (Washington, D.C., 1950), 57. The emphasis is Halder's.
2. Adolf Hitler, *Hitler's Secret Conversations 1941–1944* (New York, 1953), 142.
3. Murray, *Change in European Balance*, 322.
4. CMH, MSS #P-090, 90.
5. Matthew Cooper, *The German Army 1933–1945* (New York, 1978) 116.
6. Georg Tessin, *Verbände und Truppen der deutschen Wehrmacht und Waffen SS 1939–1945*, vol. 1 (Osnabrück, 1977), 276.
7. Quartermaster War Diary, Tenth Army, 1 September 1939, NARS T-312/77/7597776. (Hereafter cited as QM KTB/Tenth Army, 1 September 1939.)
8. CMH, MSS #P-090, 84.
9. Halder, *Halder Diaries*, vol. 2, 22.
10. Guderian, *Panzer Leader*, 71–72.
11. QM KTB/Tenth Army, 1 September 1939, NARS T-312/77/7597776.
12. QM KTB/Tenth Army, 3 September 1939, NARS T-312/77/7597777.
13. QM KTB/Tenth Army, 22 September 1939, NARS T-312/77/7597788.
14. QM KTB/Tenth Army, 27 September 1939, NARS T-312/77/7597794. This was especially true during the battle of Warsaw.
15. QM KTB/Tenth Army, 18 September 1939, NARS T-312/77/7597787.
16. CMH, MSS #P-090, 241.
17. Walther Hubatsch, *Weserübung* (Göttingen, 1960), 39.
18. Piers Mackesy, "Problems of Amphibious Power: Britain against France 1793–1815," *Naval War College Review* 30, no. 4 (Spring 1978): 20.
19. Klaus Maier and Bernd Stegmann, "Die Sicherung der europäischen Nordflanke," in Militärgeschichtlichen Forschungsamt, *Das Deutsche Reich und der Zweite Weltkrieg*, vol. 2, 201.

20. German Naval Group Command North, After-action Report on the Norwegian Campaign, 8 June 1940, NARS T-1022/2664/39876.
21. Cajus Bekker, *Hitler's Naval War* (New York, 1977), 118.
22. German Naval Group Command North, After-action Report on the Norwegian Campaign, 8 June 1940, NARS T-1022/2664/39876.
23. Williamson Murray, *Luftwaffe* (Baltimore, 1985), 38.
24. Quartermaster of Twenty-First Army Group, After-action Report on the Supplying of Troops in the Norwegian Campaign, 18 July 1940, NARS T-312/991/9183882.
25. Murray, *Change in European Balance*, 326.
26. Rolf-Dieter Müller, "Anfänge einer Reorganisation der Kriegswirtschaft am Jahrwechsel 1941/42," in Militärgeschichtlichen Forschungsamt, *Das Deutsche Reich und der Zweite Weltkrieg*, vol. 5, 630.
27. IMT, TTMWC, Doc. EC-606, vol. 36, 580–81.
28. Horst Rohde, "Hitlers ersten 'Blitzkrieg' und seine Auswirkungen auf Nordosteuropa," in Militärgeschichtlichen Forschungsamt, *Das Deutsche Reich und der Zweite Weltkrieg*, vol. 2, 133.
29. Halder, *Halder Diaries*, vol. 3, 76.
30. Ibid., 80.
31. Hardach, *First World War*, 112.
32. Halder, *Halder Diaries*, vol. 3, 128.
33. OB East, Situation Report on Economic Mobilization for the Period 27 March-14 May 1940, 22 May 1940, NARS T-501/212/000922.
34. CMH, MSS #P-090, 91.
35. Quartermaster of 31st Infantry Division, Activity Report on the Campaign in the West, (9–31 May 1940) 31 May 1940, Bundesarchiv-Militärarchiv, File RH 26-31/65. (Hereafter cited as BA-MA, RH 26-31/65).
36. Tessin, *Verbände und Truppen*, vol. 3, 143.
37. Halder, *Halder Diaries*, vol. 3, 166.
38. Report from 581st Army Supply Battalion to Quartermaster of Fourth Army on Inspection of Transport Columns of 62nd Infantry Division, 11 April 1940, NARS T-312/121/7651965.
39. Report from 581st Army Supply Battalion to Quartermaster of Fourth Army on Inspection of Transport Columns of 32nd Infantry Division, 13 April 1940, NARS T-312/121/7651963.
40. Quartermaster of Fourth Army, General Supply Directive No. 99, 7 May 1940, NARS T-312/121/7651905.
41. Quartermaster of Fourth Army, General Supply Directive No. 95, 27 April 1940, NARS T-312/121/7651935.
42. For details see Robert Allan Doughty, *The Breaking Point* (Hamden, Conn., 1990).
43. CMH, MSS #B-847, Gerd von Rundstedt, "Notes on the 1939 Polish Campaign," 1954, 2.
44. CMH, MSS #P-090, 259.
45. QM KTB/218th Infantry Division, 11 June 1940, BA-MA, RH 26-218/137.
46. QM KTB/218th Infantry Division, 7 June 1940, BA-MA, RH 26-218/137.

47. Quartermaster of Fourth Army, Directive for the Establishment and Conduct of the Supply Route, Annex to Supply Directive no. 11, 20 May 1940, NARS T-314/337/000414.

48. Martin Gareis, *Kampfe und Ende der fränkisch-sudetendeutschen 98. Infanterie-Division* (Bad Nauheim, 1956), 22–23.

49. Quartermaster of the 31st Infantry Division, Activity Report on the Campaign in the West (9–31 May 1940), 31 May 1940, BA-MA, RH 26-31/65.

50. Quartermaster of VIII Corps, Order No. 26, Special Instructions for Supply, 5 June 1940, NARS T-314/377/000541.

51. Quartermaster of Sixth Army, Special Instructions No. 8 for Supply, 8 June 1940, NARS T-312/1379/001185. The same orders were issued to the Seventh Army on 10 June 1940. Quartermaster of Seventh Army, Collection Order No. 1, 10 June 1940, NARS T-312/1521/000304.

52. QM KTB/218th Infantry Division, 16 June 1940, BA-MA, RH 26-218/137.

53. Quartermaster of Fourth Army, Report to Quartermaster of OKH, 18 June 1940, NARS T-312/121/7652873.

54. Rolf-Dieter Müller, Anfänge einer Reorganisation der Kriegswirtschaft am Jahrewechsel 1941/42," in Militärgeschichtlichen Forschungsamt, *Das Deutsche Reich und der Zweite Weltkrieg*, vol. 5, 630.

55. Maurice Pearton, *Oil and the Romanian State* (New York, 1971), 251.

56. Goralski and Freeburg, *Oil and War*, 36.

57. CMH, MSS #P-103, Hellmuth Reinhardt et al., "Utilization of Captured Material by Germany in World War II," 1953, 7.

58. QM KTB/218th Infantry Division, 22–30 June 1940, BA-MA, RH 26-218/ 137.

59. Quartermaster of Sixth Army, Special Instructions No. 8 for Supply, 8 June 1940, NARS T-312/1379/001185.

60. Quartermaster of Sixth Army, Special Instructions No. 27 for Supply, 27 June 1940, NARS T-312/1379/000826.

61. Hans Umbreit, "Auf dem Weg zur Kontinentalherrschaft," in Militärgeschichtlichen Forschungsamt, *Das Deutsche Reich und der Zweite Weltkrieg*, vol. 5, 222.

62. Karl Klee, *Das Unternehmen Seelöwe* (Göttingen, 1958), 87.

63. Ibid., 197.

64. Halder, *Halder Diaries*, vol. 4, 133.

65. Letter from Admiral Eberhart Weichold to Admiral Walter Ansel, 20 February 1953. This letter is part of Admiral Ansel's file, located at CMH.

CHAPTER 3

1. Armand de Caulaincourt, *With Napoleon in Russia* (New York, 1935), 63.

2. Quoted in Trumbull Higgins, *Hitler and Russia* (New York, 1966), 96.

3. Quartermaster of Twelfth Army, Supply Situation as of 12 April 1941, 13 April 1941, NARS T-312/445/8028272.

4. OKH Training Directive to 11th Panzer Division, 22 November 1940, NARS T-315/584/000216.

5. Percy Schramm, ed., *Kriegstagebuch des Oberkommando der Wehrmacht*, vol. 1 (Frankfurt-am-Main, 1963), 218. (Hereafter cited as KTB/OKW.)

6. Commander of German Military Mission in Romania, Special Orders for Supply for the Entry into Bulgaria, 25 January 1941, NARS T-313/2/7225530.

7. Quartermaster of First Panzer Group, Lessons in the Area of Supply from the Serbian Campaign, 22 April 1941, NARS T-313/2/7226128.

8. Quartermaster of Twelfth Army, Total Losses for Period 6–30 April 1941, 30 April 1941, NARS T-312/445/8028350.

9. QM KTB/First Panzer Group, 17 April 1941, NARS T-313/2/7225291.

10. Ernst Klink, "Die Militärische Konzeption des Krieges gegen die Sowjetunion," in Militärgeschichtlichen Forschungsamt, *Das Deutsche Reich und der Zweite Weltkrieg*, vol. 4, 262.

11. Rolf-Dieter Müller, "Das Scheiten der wirtschaftlichen 'Blitzkrieg strategic," in Militärgeschichtlichen Forschungsamt, *Das Deutsche Reich und der Zweite Weltkrieg*, vol. 4, 960.

12. USSBS, "The Effects of Strategic Bombing on the German War Economy," 74.

13. Halder, *Halder Diaries*, vol. 6, 34.

14. Ibid., 94. The diary actually says two thousand, but that undoubtedly is a misprint.

15. CMH, MSS #D-098, 2.

16. German Army, *Merkblatt für den Veterinäroffizier uber Primoplasmosen und Anaplasmosen*, 2 January 1941, NARS T-78/188/6129146.

17. Quartermaster of Fourth Army, Report on Supply Situation, 29 October 1940, NARS T-312/122/7653730.

18. Compare Quartermaster of Fourth Army, Special Order No. 21 for Supply and for the Rear Services, 11 August 1940, NARS T-312/122/7653329 with QM KTB/Tenth Army, 18 September 1939, NARS T-312/77/7597787.

19. Quartermaster of Fourth Army, Special Orders No. 7 for Supply and for the Rear Services, 18 July 1940, NARS T-312/122/7653471.

20. Quartermaster of Fourth Army, Special Orders for Supply in Each Army Area, 17 July 1940, NARS T-312/122/7653475.

21. CMH, MSS #D-099, Rudolf Nieven and Lukas Schaefer, "Remounts, Acclimatization and Breeds," n.d., 2.

22. Quartermaster of Fourth Army, General Supply Directive no. 8, 30 October 1940, NARS T-312/122/7653722.

23. Alexander Dallin, *German Rule in Russia 1941–1945*, 2d ed. (Boulder, 1981), 39.

24. Quartermaster of OKH, Special Orders for Supply, 3 April 1941, NARS T313/15/7241797.

25. Robert Conquest, *The Harvest of Sorrow* (New York, 1986), 179. It is worth noting that by 1940, the horse population of the Soviet Union was only about 21 million, still well below the pre-1928 level. Alec Nove, An Economic History of the USSR (New York, 1969), 277.

26. Supplementary Orders by Army Group Commands for the Supply of Armies and Panzer Groups, 22 May 1941, NARS T-313/15/7241818.

27. George E. Blau, *The German Campaign in Russia—Planning and Operations (1940–1942)*, (Washington, D.C., 1955), 38–40.
28. Albert Seaton, *The Russo-German War 1941–45* (New York, 1970), 56–57.
29. Ibid., 60.
30. Guderian, *Panzer Leader*, 146.
31. Blau, *Campaign in Russia*, 28.
32. Guderian, *Panzer Leader*, 147.
33. Hermann Hoth, *Panzer-Operationen* (Heidelberg, 1956), 140.
34. Blau, *Campaign in Russia*, 41.
35. Ibid.
36. Cari Wagener, *Heeresgruppe Süd* (Bad Neuheim, 1967), 23.
37. Werner Haupt, *Die Schlachten der Heeresgruppe Süd* (Darmstadt, 1985), 16.
38. Quartermaster of Fourth Army Report, 14 June 1941, NARS T-312/141/7679262.
39. CMH, MSS #P-190, Rudolf Hofmann and Alfred Toppe, "Consumption and Attrition Rates Attendant to the Operation of German Army Group Center in Russia 22 June 1941–31 December 1941," 1953, 65.
40. Seaton, *Russo-German War*, 140.
41. Goralski and Freeburg, *Oil and War*, 73.
42. USSBS, "German Motor Vehicle Industry Report," 5.
43. Rolf-Dieter Müller, "Das Scheiten der wirtschaftlichen 'Blitzkriegstrategie,," in Militärgeschichtlichen Forschungsamt, *Das Deutsche Reich und der Zweite Weltkrieg*, vol. 4, 974.
44. CMH, MSS #D-097, Kurt Seifert and Lukas Schaefer, "Horses in the Russian Campaign," 1947, 7.
45. Veterinary Officer of 21st Infantry Division, Activity Report No. 1 on the Russian Campaign (Annexes to Division KTB), 1 June-31 August 1941, BA-MA, RH 26-21/137b.
46. Omer Bartov, *The Eastern Front 1941–45: German Troops and the Barbarization of Warfare* (London, 1985), 131.
47. CMH, MSS #D-278, Unsigned, "To What Are the Heavy Losses of Horses of the Horse-Drawn Artillery in the East to Be Traced Back?" 1947, 8.
48. CMH, MSS #P-090, 262.
49. CMH, MSS #D-098, 7.
50. van Creveld, *Supplying War*, 155.
51. Bryan I. Fugate, *Operation Barbarossa* (Novato, Calif., 1984), 107–8.
52. Fridolin von Senger und Etterlin, *Die 24. Panzer-Division vormals 1. Kavallerie-Division 1939–1945* (Neckargemund, 1962), 50.
53. Veterinary Officer of 21st Infantry Division, Activity Report no. 1 on the Russian Campaign (Annexes to Division KTB), 1 June-31 August 1941, BA-MA RH 26-21/137b.
54. Veterinary Officer KTB/23rd Infantry Division, 4 August 1941, BA-MA RH 26-23/72.
55. Veterinary Officer of 44th Infantry Division, Additional Report to the Monthly Sick Report of the 44th Veterinary Company for the Month of June 1941, BA-MA RH 26-44/53.

56. Veterinary Officer of 21st Infantry Division, Lessons From the Supply Area, 27 August 1941, BA-MA RH 26-21/139a.

57. CMH, MSS #D-232, unsigned, "Condition of Railways in the Baltic Countries during the Advance of the Eighteenth Army to Leningrad," 1947, 5.

58. van Creveld, *Supplying War*, 160.

59. Horst Rohde, Das Deutsche Wehrmachttransportwesen im Zweiten Weltkrieg (Stuttgart, 1971), 321.

60. CMH, MSS #P-090, 81.

61. Earl F. Ziemke and Magna E. Bauer, *Moscow to Stalingrad: Decision in the East* (Washington, D.C., 1987), 28.

62. CMH, MSS #D-097, 6.

63. CMH, MSS #P-090, 241.

64. Veterinary Officer of 44th Infantry Division, Activity Report for Period 27 March 1941–1 December 1941, 1 December 1941, BA-MA, RH 26-44/55.

65. Veterinary Officer of 21st Infantry Division, Activity Report no. 1 on the Russian Campaign (Annexes to Division KTB), 1 June–31 August 1941, BA-MA, RH 26-21/137b.

66. CMH, MSS #D-034, Lothar Rendulic, "Diseases of Men and Horses Experienced by the Troops in Russia," 1947, 8.

67. Veterinary Officer of 30th Infantry Division, Activity Report for the Period 19 June-31 August 1941, BA-MA, RH 26-30/95.

68. John Erickson, *The Soviet High Command* (New York, 1962), 567.

69. A detailed organization for a 1941 Soviet rifle division is provided in OKH/Fremde Heeres Ost, "An Example of the Attack of a Russian Rifle Division," 20 March 1941, NARS T-78/588/000681. (Hereafter cited as OKH/FHO.)

70. Veterinary Officer of 21st Infantry Division, Activity Report no. 1 on the Russian Campaign (Annexes to Division KTB), 1 June–31 August 1941, BA-MA, RH 26-21/137b.

71. Werner Haupt, *Die 260. Infanterie-Division 1939–1944* (Dorheim, 1970), 89.

72. Nove, *Economic History of the USSR*, 285.

73. Veterinary Officer of 21st Infantry Division, Activity Report no. 1 on the Russian Campaign (Annexes to Division KTB), 1 June–31 August 1941, BA-MA, RH 26-21/137b.

74. CMH, MSS #D-278, 4–5.

75. Ibid., 5.

76. CMH, MSS #P-090, 21.

77. CMH, MSS #D-099, 6.

78. For a precise German order of battle, see Werner Haupt, *Heeresgruppe Mitte* (Dorheim, 1988), 84–86.

79. Seaton, *Russo-German War*, 180.

80. Veterinary Officer KTB/23rd Infantry Division, 2 September 1941, BA-MA, RH 26-23/76.

81. Guderian, *Panzer Leader*, 198.

82. Ibid., 233–34.

83. Quartermaster of First Panzer Army, Temporary Measures for the Advancing of Supplies, 22 October 1941, NARS T-313/15/7242362.

84. CMH, MSS #B-847, 2.

85. Veterinary Officer of 30th Infantry Division, Activity Report for the Period 1 September–30 November 1941, BA-MA RH 26-30/95.

86. OKH Report on the Combat Strength of the Eastern Army, 6 November 1941, NARS T-781335/6291878.

87. Klaus Reinhardt, *Die Wende vor Moskau* (Stuttgart, 1972), 116.

88. Seaton, *Russo-German War*, 235.

89. CMH, MSS #P-103, 7.

90. Rolf-Dieter Müller, "Das Scheiten der wirtschaften 'Blitzkriegstrategie,'" in Militärgeschichtlichen Forschungsamt, *Das Deutsche Reich und der Zweite Weltkrieg*, vol. 4, 974. The production figure comes from RWM Monthly Industrial Production Report, December 1941, NARS T-71/97/598713.

91. 5th Panzer Division, After-action Report on the Winter War of 1941/42 in Russia, 20 May 1942, NARS T-78/202/6145525.

92. 7th Infantry Division, Reply to Fourth Panzer Army Questionnaire on Lessons from the Winter, 11 May 1942, NARS T-78/202/6145627.

93. CMH, MSS #D-097, 3.

94. 7th Infantry Division, Reply to Fourth Panzer Army Questionnaire on Lessons from the Winter, 11 May 1942, NARS T-78/202/6145627.

95. XX Army Corps, Lessons in the Winter Campaign, 16 May 1942, NARS T78/202/6145562.

96. See for examples 5th Panzer Division, After-action Report on the Winter War of 1941/42 in Russia, 20 May 1942, NARS T-78/202/6145525 and IX Army Corps, After-action Report on the Winter War 1941/42, 3 July 1942, NARS T-78/ 202/6145611.

97. XX Army Corps, Lessons in the Winter Campaign, 16 May 1942, NARS T78/202/6145562.

98. Ibid.

99. Quartermaster of Fourth Army, Annex 3 to Special Order No. 103, 8 December 1941, NARS T-312/164/7706917.

100. Ziemke and Bauer, *Stalingrad to Berlin*, 51–52.

101. Report on Improvements to the Main Ready Gas Chamber in the 552nd Army Horse Hospital, May 1940, NARS T-312/1521/000230.

102. CMH, MSS #D-034, 7.

103. By 25 December 1941, the Germans had suffered some 100,000 casualties from frostbite. Peter Calvocoressi and Guy Wint, Total War (New York, 1979), 178.

104. CMH, MSS #P-090, 84.

105. Annex to Report by Quartermaster of Seventh Army, 1 April 1940, NARS T-312/1521/000729.

106. Staff Directory of First Panzer Group, 2 May 1941, NARS T-313/15/7241716.

107. Quartermaster of First Panzer Army, Report to Quartermaster of OKH, 11 December 1941, NARS T-313/26/7256555.

108. Müller-Hillebrand, *Das Heer 1933–1945*, vol. 3, 219.

109. Janusz Piekalkiewicz, *The Cavalry of World War II* (London, 1979), 244.
110. Goralski and Freeburg, *Oil and War*, 70.
111. J.F.C. Fuller, *On Future Warfare* (London, 1928), 132.
112. Quartermaster of First Panzer Army, Conference on the Supplying of Troops in the Winter, 2 November 1941, NARS T-313/26/7256509.
113. IX Army Corps, After-action Report on the Winter War 1941/42, 3 July 1942, NARS T-78/202/6145611.
114. 7th Infantry Division, Reply to Fourth Panzer Army Questionnaire on Lessons from the Winter, 11 May 1942, NARS T-78/202/6145627.
115. CMH, MSS #D-184, Walter Poppe, "Campaign of the 255th Infantry Division East and South of Temkino (December 1941–April 1942)," 1947, 19.
116. KTB/OKW, vol. 1, 489.
117. van Creveld, *Supplying War*, 142.
118. Reinhardt, *Die Wende vor Moskau*, 115.

CHAPTER 4

1. Hugh R. Trevor-Roper, *Hitler's War Directives 1939–1945* (London, 1964), 118. The emphasis is included in the original.
2. Walter Görlitz, *Paulus and Stalingrad* (1963; reprint, Westport, 1974), 276.
3. Quoted in William Craig, *Enemy at the Gates* (New York, 1973), 350.
4. Quoted in Guderian, *Panzer Leader*, 309.
5. Reinhardt, *Wende vor Moskau*, 291.
6. Seaton, *The Russo-German War*, 258.
7. Goralski and Freeburg, *Oil and War*, 177. The complete war directive is in Trevor-Roper, *Hitler's War Directives*, 116–121.
8. Tessin, *Verbände und Truppen*, vol. 3, 174.
9. Rolf Stoves, *Die 1. Panzer Division* (Bad Neuheim, 1961), 342.
10. Blau, *The German Campaign in Russia-Planning and Operations*, 137.
11. CMH, MSS #P-090, 91.
12. CMH, MSS #D-097, 5.
13. Veterinary Officer of Sixth Army, Report, 22 June 1942, NARS T-312/1448/000042.
14. QM KTB/First Panzer Army, 10 June 1942, NARS T-313/43/7276610.
15. The precise dates for the changes in nomenclature are as follows: The First and Second Panzer Groups were redesignated as Panzer Armies on 6 October 1941. KTB/OKW, vol. 1, 681. The Third and Fourth Panzer Groups were redesignated as Panzer Armies on 2 January 1942, KTB/OKW, vol. 2, 187.
16. Liddell-Hart, *History of the Second World War*, 251.
17. Dallin, *German Rule in Russia*, 243.
18. Goralski and Freeburg, *Oil and War*, 182–83.
19. Veterinary Officer of Sixth Army, Report to Quartermaster of Sixth Army on Horse Matters in the Divisions, 9 July 1942, NARS T-312/1448/000484.
20. CMH, MSS #D-278, 10.

21. Quartermaster of Sixth Army, Estimate of Supply Situation, 28 July 1942, NARS T-312/1449/000162.

22. B. H. Liddell-Hart, *The German Generals Talk* (New York, 1948), 202.

23. Craig, *Enemy at the Gates*, 118.

24. Quartermaster of Sixth Army, Report on Supply Situation to Quartermaster of OKH, 21 October 1942, NARS T-312/1450/000435.

25. Veterinary Officer of Sixth Army to 541st Army Horse Park, 4 September 1942, NARS T-312/1449/000397.

26. Quartermaster of Sixth Army, Preparations for the Winter of 1942/1943, 14 September 1942, NARS T-312/1449/000572.

27. Quartermaster of Sixth Army, Report on Supply Situation to Quartermaster of OKH, 9 November 1942, NARS T-312/1450/000906.

28. Veterinary Officer of Sixth Army to All Corps, 16 November 1942, NARS T312/1450/001071.

29. This is certainly implied by Seaton, *The Russo-German War*, 338–40.

30. This is a best estimate. By mid-December the Sixth Army had almost 24,000 horses in Stalingrad. Some horses had already been slaughtered for food as early as November.

31. Louis Rotondo, ed., *Battle for Stalingrad* (New York, 1989), 316–17.

32. Ibid., 160.

33. Quartermaster of Sixth Army, Estimate of Supply Situation, 28 July 1942, NARS T-312/1449/000162.

34. OKH/FHO, Table of Organization and Equipment for a Russian Infantry Division, 15 July 1942, NARS T-78/550/000936.

35. OKH/FHO, Presumed War Organization of a Rifle Division as of 10 December 1942, June 1944, NARS T-78/580/000226.

36. Murray, *Luftwaffe*, 146–48.

37. Craig, *Enemy at the Gates*, 227.

38. Erich von Manstein, *Lost Victories*, (1958; Reprint, Novato, 1982), 337.

39. Görlitz, *Paulus and Stalingrad*, 276.

40. Murray, *Luftwaffe*, 148.

41. See for example QM KTB/Sixth Army, 19 December 1942, NARS T-312/1451/000210.

42. Quartermaster of Army Group Don, Telegram to Quartermaster of Sixth Army, 14 December 1942, NARS T-312/1451/000129.

43. QM KTB/Sixth Army, 16 January 1943, NARS T-312/1451/000527.

44. Craig, *Enemy at the Gates*, 360.

45. Ibid., 350.

46. Seaton, *The Russo-German War*, 335.

47. Cooper, *The German Army*, 433–34.

48. QM KTB/First Panzer Army, 20 September 1942, NARS T-313/43/7276694.

49. See for example Quartermaster of First Panzer Army, Report on Animal Situation, 19 February 1943, NARS T-313/49/7283829.

50. Wilhelm Tieke, *Der Kaukasus und das Öl* (Osnabrück, 1970), 495.

51. Organization Section of OKH, Table on Truck Production, 30 September 1943, NARS T-78/413/6382018.

52. Pearton, *Oil and the Romanian State*, 261–62.

53. Seaton, *The Russo-German War*, 358.
54. Ernst Klink, *Das Gesetz des Handelns: Die Operation "Zitadelle" 1943* (Stuttgart, 1966), 122.
55. Quartermaster of Fourth Panzer Army, Estimate of Supply Situation, 4 May 1943, NARS T-313/386/8675833.
56. Quartermaster of Fourth Panzer Army, Estimate of Supply Situation, 3 June 1943, NARS T-313/386/8675877.
57. Quartermaster of Ninth Army, Supply Situation Report, 1 August 1943, NARS T-312/316/7884492.
58. Earl F. Ziemke, *Stalingrad to Berlin: The German Defeat in the East* (Washington, D.C., 1968), 170.
59. Veterinary Officer of Eighth Army, Report to Quartermaster of Eighth Army, 3 October 1943, NARS T-312/62/7579548.
60. Veterinary Officer of First Panzer Army, Activity Report for Period 1–31 January 1944, 5 May 1944, NARS T-313/75/7313434.
61. Quartermaster of XXIV Panzer Corps, Report on Supply Situation to Quartermaster of Eighth Army, 2 October 1943, NARS T-312/62/7579599.
62. Ziemke, *Stalingrad to Berlin*, 172.
63. Haupt, *Heeresgruppe Mitte*, 195.
64. Ziemke, *Stalingrad to Berlin*, 172.

CHAPTER 5
1. Friedrich Ruge, "The Invasion of Normandy," in Hans-Adolf Jacobsen and Jürgen Rohwer, eds., *Decisive Battles of World War II: The German View* (New York, 1965), 323.
2. Louis P. Lochner, ed., *The Goebbels Diaries 1942–1943* (New York, 1948), 434.
3. Hans Umbreit, "Auf dem Weg zur Kontinentalherrschaft," in Militärgeschichtlichen Forschungsamt, *Das Deutsche Reich und der Zweite Weltkrieg*, vol. 5, 232.
4. Veterinary Officer of VIII Corps, Activity Report for the Period 1–31 January 1942, 6 February 1942, NARS T-314/384/000217.
5. CMH, MSS #D-099, 2.
6. Samuel W. Mitcham, Jr., *Hitler's Legions* (New York, 1985), 248–49.
7. Quartermaster of LXXXI Corps, Activity Report for the Period 15–30 April 1942, 3 May 1942, NARS T-314/1584/000769.
8. van Creveld, *Fighting Power* (Westport, Conn., 1982), 99.
9. Görlitz, *Paulus and Stalingrad*, 272.
10. KTB/295th Infantry Division, 29 April 1943, NARS T-315/1952/000690.
11. Nove, *Economic History of the USSR*, 285.
12. Halder, *Halder Diaries*, vol. 3, 128.
13. Brian Mitchell, *European Historical Statistics 1750–1975*, 2d rev. ed. (New York, 1981), 335.
14. CMH, MSS #P-090, 235.
15. Ibid., 16.

16. Werner Warmbrunn, *The Dutch under German Occupation 1940–1945* (Stanford, 1963), 72.
17. Netherlands Central Bureau of Statistics, *Historical Series of the Netherlands 1899–1984* (The Hague, 1985), 95.
18. Earl R. Beck, *Under the Bombs*(Lexington, Mass., 1986), 147.
19. DiNardo and Bay, "Horse-Drawn Transport," 133.
20. Liddell-Hart, *German Generals Talk*, 232.
21. Tessin, *Verbände und Truppen*, vol. 5, 176.
22. Ibid.
23. Quartermaster of LXVIII Corps, Instructions on the Arrangement of Winter Quarters and Camps in the Peleponese, 29 July 1943, NARS T-314/1540/ 000586.
24. Mitcham, *Hitler,s Legions*, 427.
25. Albert Seaton, *The German Army 1933–45* (New York, 1982), 202.
26. Quartermaster of LXXXI Corps, Report, 4 March 1944, NARS T-314/1591/000024.
27. Murray, *Luftwaffe*, 116.
28. Jürgen Forster, "The Dynamics of Volksgemeinschaft: The Effectiveness of the German Military Establishment in the Second World War," in Millett and Murray, eds., *Military Effectiveness*, vol. 3, 190.
29. Seaton, *Russo-German War*, 399.
30. By the end of July 1944, seven of these eleven divisions were still in action, three had been destroyed and were to be disbanded, while one was scheduled to be refit. OKH, Summary of Large Units of the Army, Waffen SS and the Parachute Troops as of 30 July 1944, 31 July 1944, NARS T-78/413/6381074.
31. RWM, The Activity of the Enemy Air Forces over the Area of the Reich in September 1944, 8 December 1944, NARS T-71/99/599643.
32. Special Report from Quartermaster of Army Group B to OKH on Production and Allocation of Italian Vehicles, 17 November 1943, NARS T-311/5/7005087.
33. Veterinary Officer of Tenth Army, Activity Report for the Period 1 January-14 February 1944, 29 February 1944, NARS T-312/88/7611485.
34. Veterinary Officer of Fourteenth Army, Report, 7 January 1944, NARS T312/485/8075919.
35. CMH, MSS #D-099, 5.
36. Carlo D'Este, *Bitter Victory* (New York, 1988), 478.
37. William F. Ross and Charles F. Romanus, *The Quartermaster Corps: Operations in the War against Germany* (Washington, D.C., 1965), 238.
38. Ibid., 240–41.
39. CMH, MSS #P-090, 221.
40. Beck, *Under the Bombs*, 147.
41. CMH, MSS #P-090, 229.
42. Beck, *Under the Bombs*, 147.

CHAPTER 6
1. Unsigned, "Das Pferd in Heer und Wirtschaft von heute," *Militär Wochenblatt* 121, no. 41, (23 April 1937), 2539.

2. 1st Cavalry Division, After-action Report of the 1st Cavalry Division on the Campaign in Holland and France, 13 August 1940, NARS T-315/83/000336. Feldt had commanded the 1st Cavalry Brigade in Poland. Wolf Keilig, *Das Deutsche Heer 1939–1945*, vol. 3, sect. 211, (Bad Neuheim, 1963), 82. The emphasis in this quote is Feldt's.

3. 1st Cavalry Division to OKH, Conversion of the 1st Cavalry Division to a Panzer-Division, 13 September 1941, NARS T-315/82/000344. The emphasis in this quote is Feldt's.

4. Norman Stone, *The Eastern Front 1914–1917* (New York, 1975), 48.

5. Ibid., 106.

6. Seaton, *German Army*, 4.

7. Hans von Luck, *Panzer Commander* (New York, 1989), 8.

8. Guderian, *Panzer Leader*, 18–24.

9. Von Poseck was an old officer, born 1 October 1865. He had served in the cavalry from his entry into the Imperial Army on 14 April 1885. Keilig, *Das Deutsche Heer*, vol. 3, sect. 211, 254.

10. Maximilian von Poseck, "Kavallerie von einst und jetzt," *Militär Wochenblatt*, 118, no. 43 (18 May 1934): 1467.

11. See Maximilian von Poseck, "Aus grosser Zeit vor zwanzig Jahren. Kriegserfahrungen in der Verwendung moderner Kavallerie," *Militär Wochenblatt* 119, no. 30, (11 February 1935): 1171–75, and the follow-up article of the same title in *Militär Wochenblatt* 119, no. 31, (18 February 1935): 1211–13.

12. Guderian, "Heereskavallerie und motorisierte Verbände," *Militär Wochenblatt* 119, no. 34, (11 March 1935): 1338–39.

13. Guderian, *Panzer Leader*, 30.

14. Murray, *Change in European Balance*, 35.

15. Richard Brett-Smith, *Hitler's Generals* (San Rafael), 164–82.

16. Murray, "British Military Effectiveness in the Second World War," in Millett and Murray, eds., *Military Effectiveness*, vol. 3, 111.

17. CMH, MSS #P-090, 215.

18. Görlitz, *History of German General Staff*, 300.

19. Fridolin von Senger und Etterlin, *Die Panzergrenadiere* (Munich, 1961), 69–70.

20. Heinz Guderian, "Schnell Truppen einst und jetzt," *Militärwissenschaftliche Rundschau* 4, no. 2, (March 1939): 242.

21. 7th Panzer Division, After-action Report of the 7th Panzer Division (formerly the 2nd Light Division), 19 October 1939, NARS T-315/436/000480.

22. von Senger und Etterlin, *Die 24. Panzer-Division vormals 1. Kavellerie-Division 1939–1945* (Neckargemund, 1962), 19.

23. CMH, MSS #B-847, 1.

24. 1st Cavalry Division, After-action Report of the 1st Cavalry Division on the Campaign in Holland and France, 13 August 1940, NARS T-315/83/000336.

25. Fridolin von Senger und Etterlin, *Neither Fear nor Hope* (New York, 1964), 22.

26. 1st Cavalry Division, After-action Report of the 1st Cavalry Division on the Campaign in Holland and France, 13 August 1940, NARS T-315/83/000336.

27. George H. Stein, *The Waffen SS* (Ithaca, N.Y., 1966), 121.

28. Ibid.

29. Haupt, *Heeresgruppe Mitte*, 25.

30. 1st Cavalry Division to OKH, Conversion of the 1st Cavalry Division to a Panzer-Division, 13 September 1941, NARS T-315/82/000344.

31. Guderian, *Panzer Leader*, 161.

32. 1st Cavalry Division, Short Report on Missions Undertaken by 1st Cavalry Division for the XXIV Panzer Corps and the XII Army Corps in the Period 1–31 July 1941, 30 July 1941, NARS T-315/82/000185.

33. 1st Cavalry Division, Report on Missions Undertaken by 1st Cavalry Division for the Second Army, XII, XIII and XLIII Army Corps for the Period 1 August-2 September 1941, 12 September 1941, NARS T-315/82/000324.

34. 1st Cavalry Division to OKH, Conversion of the 1st Cavalry Division to a Panzer-Division, 13 September 1941, NARS T-315/82/000344.

35. 1st Cavalry Division, Activity Report for the Period 8 November 1941–29 April 1942, 29 April 1942, NARS T-315/83/000214.

36. Seaton, *German Army*, 202.

37. von Senger und Etterlin, *Neither Fear nor Hope*, 108.

38. James Lucas, *War on the Eastern Front 1941–1945* (New York, 1982), 114.

39. 8th SS Cavalry Division (Florian Geyer), Division Table of Organization and Equipment as of 21 June 1942, NARS T-354/640/000006. The Division was later reinforced with another two cavalry regiments, giving it a total of four, organized into two brigades. Mitcham, *Hitler,s Legions*, 449.

40. Stein, *Waffen SS*, 275.

41. Dallin, *German Rule in Russia*, 298–99.

42. Jürgen Thorwald, *The Illusion* (New York, 1975), 142.

43. Ibid., 177–78.

44. Lucas, *War on the Eastern Front*, 115.

45. Mitcham, *Hitler's Legions*, 474.

46. Jürgen E. Forster, "The Dynamics of Volksgemeinschaft: The Effectiveness of the German Military Establishment in the Second World War," in Millett and Murray, eds., *Military Effectiveness*, vol. 3, 211.

47. SS Cavalry Brigade, Training Instructions for the Remaining Units of the SS Cavalry Brigade, 9 September 1942, NARS T-354/641/000021.

48. 1st SS Cavalry Regiment, Training Plan for All Squadrons for the Period 11–13 April 1943, 11 April 1943, NARS T-354/643/000596.

49. 1st SS Cavalry Regiment, Training Plan for the Heavy Machine Gun Squadron for the Period 21–27 March 1943, 22 March 1943, NARS T-354/643/000654.

50. QM KTB/Cavalry Corps, 1 June 1944, NARS T-314/26/000772.

51. Cavalry Corps, Organization of Group Harteneck, 4 July 1944, NARS T314/25/000362.

52. Quartermaster of First Panzer Army, Veterinary Section Activity Report for the Period 1–31 January 1944, 5 May 1944, NARS T-313/75/7313434.

53. Quartermaster of First Panzer Army, Veterinary Section Activity Report for the Period 1–29 February 1944, 6 May 1944, NARS T-313/75/7313441.

54. Quartermaster of First Panzer Army, Veterinary Section Activity Report for the Period 1–31 March 1944, 7 May 1944, NARS T-313/75/7313446.

55. Cavalry Corps, Organization Chart of the Cavalry Corps, 23 July 1944, NARS T-314/25/000862.

56. Commanding General of Cavalry Corps, Report to the Commander of the Second Army on the Further Employment of the Hungarian Cavalry Division in the Sector of the Cavalry Corps, 5 August 1944, NARS T-314/25/001009.

57. Cavalry Corps, Organization Chart of the Cavalry Corps, 4 August 1944, NARS T-314/25/001004.

58. Quartermaster of Cavalry Corps, Special Order for Supply No. 2, 15 August 1944, NARS T-314/26/000857.

59. Quartermaster of Cavalry Corps, Special Order for Supply No. 11, 9 November 1944, NARS T-314/27/000954.

60. Quartermaster of Cavalry Corps, Report to the Quartermaster of Fourth Army on Comments on Condition Report, 10 November 1944, NARS T-314/27/ 000961.

61. Mitcham, *Hitler's Legions*, 449.

62. Thorwald, *The Illusion*, 316.

63. KTB/Cavalry Corps, 31 December 1944, NARS T-314/27/000053. This was the last day of the Cavalry Corps as an operational entity.

CHAPTER 7

1. Dwight D. Eisenhower, *Crusade in Europe* (New York, 1951), 279.

2. The Soviets refer to it as the battle of Korsun. German sources call it the battle of the Cherkassy pocket. Ziemke, *Stalingrad to Berlin*, 226.

3. Wagener, *Heeresgruppe Süd*, 269.

4. Paul Carell, *Scorched Earth* (Boston, 1970), 398.

5. John Erickson, *The Road to Berlin* (Boulder, 1983), 179.

6. Carell, *Scorched Earth*, 432.

7. Wagener, *Heeresgruppe Süd*, 273.

8. Department of the Army, Pamphlet #20–234, Operations of Encircled Forces (Washington, D.C., 1952), 32.

9. Ziemke, *Stalingrad to Berlin*, 275.

10. Seaton, *Russo-German War*, 431.

11. Piekalkiewicz, *Cavalry of World War II*, 227.

12. Dieter Ose, *Entscheidung im Westen 1944* (Stuttgart, 1982), 70–71.

13. Alan S. Milward, *The German Economy at War* (London, 1965), 119.

14. Pearton, *Oil and the Romanian State*, 261–62.

15. Goralski and Freeburg, *Oil and War*, 269.

16. Supplement to Memorandum from Quartermaster Staff of Army Group B to Operations Section, 29 May 1944, NARS T-311/1/7000636.

17. CMH, MSS #B-007, Kurt Badinski, "276th Infantry Division (1 January–20 August 1944)," 1946, 3–4.

18. CMH, MSS #B-403, Joseph Reichert, "711th Infantry Division (1 April 1943–24 July 1944)," 15.

19. Ibid., 3–4.

20. CMH, MSS #B-432, Lieutenant Colonel Fritz Ziegelmann, "352nd Infantry Division (5 December 1943–6 June 1944)," 1946, 5.

21. CMH, MSS #B-540, Friedrich Schack, "272nd Infantry Division (15 December 1943–26 July 1944)," 1947, 2.

22. For a complete order of battle, see Ose, *Entscheidung im Westen 1944*, 95–98.

23. Army Group B, Supply Situation in Area of OB West, Part of Material Used for Report to Hitler, March 1944, NARS T-311/1/7000476.

24. For details see Murray, *Luftwaffe*, 198–247.

25. Russell F. Weigley, *Eisenhower's Lieutenants* (Bloomington, Ind., 1981), 67.

26. QM KTB/Army Group B, 11 May 1944, NARS T-311/1/7000575.

27. Dieter Ose, "Rommel and Rundstedt: The 1944 Panzer Controversy," *Military Affairs* 50, no. 1 (January 1986), 9.

28. Rommel's subordination to Rundstedt was only theoretical because as a field marshal, Rommel had equal access to Hitler and could thus go over Rundstedt's head.

29. See Quartermaster of Fourteenth Army, Estimate of Supply Situation, 3 May 1944, NARS T-312/485/8076722 and Quartermaster of Fourteenth Army, Situation Report to Operations Officer of Fourteenth Army, 22 June 1944, NARS T312/486/8077504.

30. Fritz Bayerlin, "Invasion—1944," in B. H. Liddell-Hart, ed., *The Rommel Papers* (New York, 1953), 466–70.

31. Ruge, "Invasion of Normandy," in Jacobsen and Rohwer, eds., *Decisive Battles*, 330.

32. Ibid.

33. Ose, "Rommel and Rundstedt," 10.

34. Ibid., 7.

35. Müller-Hillebrand, *Das Heer*, vol. 1, 71–73.

36. G. A. Shepperd, *The Italian Campaign 1943–45* (London, 1968), 396–97.

37. Bayerlin, in Liddell-Hart, *The Rommel Papers*, 468.

38. Veterinary Officer KTB/Seventh Army, 19 June 1944, NARS T-312/1571/000519.

39. Veterinary Officer KTB/Seventh Army, 26 June 1944, NARS T-312/1571/000566.

40. Veterinary Officer KTB/Seventh Army, 28 June 1944, NARS T-312/1571/000577.

41. CMH, MSS #B-007, 7–7a.

42. CMH, MSS #B-424, Kurt Schuster, "85th Infantry Division (31 July-8 August 1944)," 1947, 5–6.

43. For details see Gordon A. Harrison, *Cross-Channel Attack* (Washington, D.C., 1951), 378–79.

44. CMH, MSS #C-024, Fritz Kramer, "I SS Panzer Corps in the West (1944)," 1948, 42.

45. Quartermaster of Seventh Army, Activity Report for Period 1–15 May 1944, 24 May 1944, NARS T-312/1571/000437.

46. Quartermaster of Army Group B, Estimate of Supply Situation of Seventh Army, 21 June 1944, NARS T-311/1/7000720.

47. CMH, MSS #B-464, Fritz Ziegelmann, "352nd Infantry Division (19–24 July 1944)," n.d., 2.

48. CMH, MSS #A-985, Paul Mahlmann, "353rd Infantry Division (11–21 August 1944)," 1946, 20.

49. Ibid.

50. CMH, MSS #B-370, Hans Schmidt, "275th Infantry Division (31 July–12 August 1944)," n.d., 18.

51. CMH, MSS #B-532, Paul Frank, "346th Infantry Division (24 July–15 September 1944)," 1946, 24–25.

52. CMH, MSS #A-986, Paul Mahlmann, "353rd Infantry Division (21 August–7 September 1944)," 1948, 38.

53. Ruge, "Invasion of Normandy," in Jacobsen and Rohwer, eds., *Decisive Battles*, 346.

54. Veterinary Officer of Seventh Army, Activity Report no. 11 for Period 1–30 June 1944, 30 June 1944, NARS T-312/1571/000848.

55. KTB/Army Group B, 15 July 1944, NARS T-311/3/7002342.

56. van Creveld, *Supplying War*, 222.

57. Weigley, *Eisenhower's Lieutenants*, 214.

58. Erickson, *Road to Berlin*, 214.

59. Seaton, *Russo-German War*, 436.

60. Fourth Army, After-action Report on the Winter Battles of 1943/1944, 6 April 1944, NARS T-311/224/000151.

61. Seaton, *Russo-German War*, 589.

62. USSBS, "German Motor Vehicle Industry Report," 17.

63. Ziemke, *Stalingrad to Berlin*, 241.

64. Ibid., 319.

65. Haupt, *Heeresgruppe Mitte*, 201–3.

66. Rolf Hinze, *Der Zusammenbruch der Heeresgruppe Mitte im Osten 1944* (Stuttgart, 1980), 20.

67. Quartermaster of Second Army, Horse Situation of Second Army, 20 June 1944, NARS T-312/1306/000330.

68. Hinze, *Zusammembruch der Heeresgruppe*, 278–86. It should be admitted, however, that the figure arrived at may well be on the low side. It is also worth noting that Hinze omits the Second Army from his order of battle for Army Group Center. An order of battle for the Second Army is included in Haupt, *Heeresgruppe Mitte*, 203.

69. Ziemke, *Stalingrad to Berlin*, 277.

70. Hermann Gackenholz, "The Collapse of Army Group Center in 1944," in Jacobsen and Rohwer, eds. *Decisive Battles*, 380.

71. Quartermaster of Second Army, Estimate of Supply Situation, 23 June 1944, NARS T-312/1306/000341.
72. Ziemke, *Stalingrad to Berlin*, 325.
73. Hinze, Zusammenbruch der Heeresgruppe, 281.
74. Haupt, *Die 260*, 235–36.
75. Gackenholz, "Collapse of Army Group Center," in Jacobsen and Rohwer, eds., *Decisive Battles*, 382.
76. Charles B. MacDonald, *A Time for Trumpets* (New York, 1985), 34.
77. Ibid., 37–38.
78. Goralski and Freeburg, *Oil and War*, 292.
79. Hasso von Manteuffel, "The Battle of the Ardennes 1944–45," in Jacobsen and Rohwer, eds., *Decisive Battles*, 400.
80. MacDonald, *Time for Trumpets*, 37.
81. Hugh M. Cole, *The Ardennes: Battle of the Bulge* (Washington, D.C., 1965), 77.
82. James Weingartner, *Crossroads of Death* (Berkeley, 1979), 47.
83. Cole, *Ardennes*, 173.
84. Even though these divisions were now called "volks grenadier," the term infantry is used here for the sake of simplicity.
85. CMH, MSS #B-040, Heinz Kokott, "26th Volks Grenadier Division in the Ardennes Offensive," n.d., 37.
86. Ibid., 45.
87. Ibid., 41.
88. Goralski and Freeburg, *Oil and War*, 299.
89. Fifteenth Army, Special Order to LXXXI Corps, 16 December 1944, NARS T-314/1594/000437.
90. Quoted in Liddell-Hart, *German Generals Talk*, 292.
91. von Senger und Etterlin, *Die Panzergrenadiere*, 226–28.
92. Basic Organizations and Special Organizations of SS Units, 15 February 1945, NARS T-354/116/3750050.
93. CMH, MSS #B-716, Percy Schramm, "Wehrmacht Losses," n.d., 8.

CHAPTER 8

1. This was a film made by Frank Capra as part of the *Why We Fight* series.
2. From the film *Patton* (1970).
3. Charles B. MacDonald, *The Mighty Endeavor* (1969; reprint, New York, 1986), 347.
4. Many thanks to that superb soldier and historian, Sir Michael Howard, for kindly taking time out from his own hectic schedule to discuss this topic with me over lunch at Yale University on 19 December 1989.
5. Joachim C. Fest, *Hitler* (New York, 1975), 393.
6. Robert Edwin Herzstein, *The War That Hitler Won* (New York, 1987), 224.
7. David Welch, "Goebbels, Gotterdammerung and the Deutsche Wochenschauen," K.R.M. Short and Stephan Dolezel, eds., *Hitler's Fall: The Newsreel Witness* (New York, 1988), 83.
8. Herzstein, *War That Hitler Won*, 232.
9. Ibid., 227.

10. John W. Dower, *War without Mercy* (New York, 1986), 77–93.
11. The list includes Erich von Stroheim, Christopher Plummer, and, most commonly, James Mason.
12. It is important to point out that the Italian Army, even though short of transportation, required comparatively few motor vehicles in North Africa as the size of the forces committed there was rather small. By August 1941, for example, the Italian Army in North Africa had 8,500 trucks. While this was somewhat less than what was required ideally, it was still sufficient to allow operations to be conducted. MacGregor Knox, "The Italian Armed Forces, 1940–3," in Millett and Murray, eds. *Military Effectiveness*, vol. 3, 166. It should all be pointed out that in the rugged terrain of East Africa, Italian forces were supplied by a well-organized and well-run pack mule service. Barrie Pitt, *The Crucible of War: Western Desert 1941* (London, 1980), 209.
13. William Manchester, *American Caesar* (New York, 1978), 791.
14. MacDonald, *The Mighty Endeavor*, 347.
15. Charles B. MacDonald, *The Battle of the Huertgen Forest* (New York, 1963), 21.
16. Carlo D'Este, *Decision in Normandy* (New York, 1983), 431.

CONCLUSION
1. From *King Richard III*, V, iv, 7.
2. These units were initially designated simply as "army corps." Later on the term motorized was used as well as panzer, but after 1942 only panzer was employed as the designation. Seaton, *German Army*, 135.
3. CMH, MSS #B-036, Hasso von Manteuffel, "Mobile and Panzer Troops," 1945, 11–12.
4. Organization of Korpsgruppe Fischer as of 9 January 1943, NARS T-315/570/ 000318.
5. CMH, MSS #P-090, 108.
6. CMH, MSS #P-080, Hellmuth Reinhardt, "The Training of Senior Officers," 1951, 10.
7. CMH, MSS #B-847, 2.
8. CMH, MSS #P-103, 7.
9. Even later in the war the German Army had to rely on civilian trucks. Ziemke, *Stalingrad to Berlin*, 241–42.
10. 7th Infantry Division, Reply to Fourth Panzer Army Questionnaire on Lessons from the Winter, 11 May 1942, NARS T-78/202/6145627.
11. Wagener, *Heeresgruppe Süd*, 178.
12. Jehuda L. Wallach, *The Dogma of the Battle of Annihilation* (Westport, Conn., 1986), 312.
13. Paddy Griffith, *Forward into Battle* (New York, 1981), 88.
14. One might notice that neither England nor Norway are included in this list. Norway is omitted, as is Denmark, because that campaign was relatively minor. The British Army was small enough so that the British Expeditionary Force (BEF) in 1940 was completely motorized, but did not play a major part in the campaign.
15. Doughty, *Breaking Point*, 321–32.

16. Sir Winston Churchill, *The Second World War*, vol. 3, (Boston, 1950), 606.

17. Reichs-Kredit-Gesellschaft, *Treibstoffwirtschaft in der Welt und in Deutschland*, c. 1939, NARS T-84/51/1332658.

18. Gordon Wright, *France in Modern Times*, 3d ed. (New York, 1981), 368–69.

19. A. J. P. Taylor, *English History 1914–1945* (Oxford, 1965), 343.

20. Reichs-Kredit-Gesellschaft, *Treibstoffwirtschaft in der Welt und in Deutschland*, c. 1939, NARS T-84/51/1332658.

21. Alan S. Milward, *The German Economy at War* (London, 1965), 110.

22. Ibid., 111.

23. If one wanted to, one could argue from this that the Allies actually profited from the fall of France, in that it cut a lot of "fat" from the alliance. That, however, would be stretching a sound argument to the point of sheer perversity. For all the failings of the French Army, and there were many, the Germans gained tremendous advantages from the occupation of France and the Low Countries.

24. Goralski and Freeburg, *Oil and War*, 338.

Bibliography

DOCUMENTARY SOURCES
National Archives Microfilmed German Records
Series T-71: Ministry of Economics
Series T-77: Armed Forces High Command
Series T-78: Army High Command
Series T-79: Military Districts
Series T-84: Miscellaneous Documents
Series T-175: Office of the Reichsführer
SS Series T-311: Army Groups
Series T-312: Field Armies
Series T-313: Panzer Groups and Armies
Series T-314: Corps
Series T-315: Divisions
Series T-354: SS Units
Series T-501: Areas of Military Occupation
Series T-1022: German Navy

Selected Documents from the Bundesarchiv-Militärarchiv, Freiburg-im-Briesgau, Germany
12th Infantry Division: File RH 26-12/131
21st Infantry Division: File RH 26-21/137b, 139a
23rd Infantry Division: File RH 26-23/72, 76
30th Infantry Division: File RH 26-30/95
31st Infantry Division: File RH 26-31/65, 71
44th Infantry Division: File RH 26-44/155, 53
218th Infantry Division: File RH 26-218/137
International Military Tribunal (IMT). Trial of the Major War Criminals, 42
    vols.
Nuremberg: U.S. Government, 1947–49.
Schramm, Percy Ernst, ed. Kriegstagebuch des Oberkommando der
    Wehrmacht. 4 vols. Frankfurt-am-Main: Bernard und Graefe für
    Wehrwesen, 1963.
U.S. Military Attaché Reports from Germany, 1920–1941.

UNPUBLISHED MANUSCRIPTS FROM THE CENTER FOR MILITARY HISTORY

MSS #A-885, Kurt Schuster. "The LXIV Corps from August to November 1944." 1946.

MSS #A-984, Paul Mahlmann. "353rd Infantry Division (24 July–10 August 1944)." 1946.

MSS #A-985, Paul Mahlmann. "353rd Infantry Division (11–21 August 1944)." 1946.

MSS #A-986, Paul Mahlmann. "353rd Infantry Division (21 August–7 September 1944)." 1948.

MSS #B-007, Kurt Badinski. "276th Infantry Division (1 January–20 August 1944)," 1946.

MSS #B-008, Paul Frank. "346th Infantry Division (February–24 July 1944)." 1946.

MSS #B-014, Hans-Kurt Höcker. "17th Luftwaffe Field Division (Pre-Invasion-24 July 1944)." 1946.

CMH, MSS #B-036, Hasso von Manteuffel. "Mobile and Panzer Troops." 1945.

MSS #B-040, Heinz Kokott. "26th Volks Grenadier Division in the Ardennes Offensive." n.d.

MSS #B-370, Hans Schmidt. "275th Infantry Division (31 July–12 August 1944)." n.d.

MSS #B-403, Joseph Reichert. "711th Infantry Division (1 April 1943–24 July 1944)." 1947.

MSS # B-424, Kurt Schuster, "85th Infantry Division (31 July–8 August 1944)." 1947.

MSS #B-432, Fritz Ziegelmann. "352nd Infantry Division (5 December 1943–6 June 1944)." 1946.

MSS #B-464, Fritz Ziegelmann. "352nd Infantry Division (19–24 July 1944)." n.d.

MSS #B-532, Paul Frank, "352nd Infantry Division (24 July–15 September 1944)." 1946.

MSS #B-540, Friedrich Schack. "272nd Infantry Division (15 December 1943–26 July 1944)." 1947.

MSS #B-716, Percy Schramm, "Wehrmacht Losses." n.d.

MSS #B-847, Gerd von Rundstedt. "Notes on the 1939 Polish Campaign." 1954.

MSS #C-024, Fritz Kramer. "I SS Panzer Corps in the West (1944)." 1948.

MSS #D-034, Lothar Rendulic. "Diseases of Men and Horses Experienced by the Troops in Russia." 1947.

MSS #D-097, Kurt Seifert and Lukas Schaefer. "Horses in the Russian Campaign." 1947.

MSS #D-098, Maximilian Betzer. "Horse Diseases during the Eastern Campaign (1941–1945)." n.d.

MSS #D-099, Rudolf Nieven and Lukas Schaefer. "Remounts, Acclimatization and Breeds." n.d.

MSS #D-184, Walter Poppe. "Campaign of the 255th Infantry Division East and South of Temkino (December 1941–April 1942)." 1947.

MSS #D-232, unsigned. "Condition of Railways in the Baltic Countries during the Advance of the Eighteenth Army to Leningrad." 1947.

MSS #D-278, unsigned. "To What are the Heavy Losses on Horses of the Horse-Drawn Artillery in the East to be Traced Back?" 1947.

MSS #D-285, Rudolf von Roman. "The 35th Infantry Division between Moscow and Gzhatsk, 1941." 1947.

MSS #P-080, Hellmuth Reinhardt. "The Training of Senior Officers." 1951.

MSS #P-090, Burkhart Müller-Hillebrand. "Horses in the German Army (1941–1945)." 1952.

MSS #P-103, Hellmuth Reinhardt et al. "Utilization of Captured Material by Germany in World War II." 1953.

MSS #P-190, Rudolf Hofmann and Alfred Toppe. "Consumption and Attrition Rates Attendant to the Operation of German Army Group Center in Russia 22 June–31 December 1941." 1953.

PUBLISHED WORKS

Addington, Larry, *The Blitzkrieg Era and the German General Staff.* New Brunswick, Rutgers University Press, 1971.

Ash, Bernard. *Norway 1940.* London: Cassell and Company, 1964.

Barnett, Corelli, ed. *Hitler's Generals.* New York: Grove Weidenfeld, 1989.

Bartov, Omer. *The Eastern Front 1941–45: German Troops and the Barbarization of Warfare.* London: The Macmillan Press, 1985.

Beck, Earl R. *Under the Bombs.* Lexington: The University Press of Kentucky, 1986.

Bekker, Cajus. *Hitler's Naval War.* New York: Zebra Books, 1977.

Belgium, Ministry of Economic Affairs. *Annuaire Statistique de la Belgique et du Congo Belge.* Vols. 66–68, 62, 1940, 1944, 1946.

Blau, George E. *The German Campaign in the Balkans (Spring 1941).* Washington, D.C.: Department of the Army, 1953.

———. *The German Campaign in Russia—Planning and Operations (1940–1942).* Washington, D.C.: Department of the Army, 1955.

Bramsted, Ernest K. *Goebbels and National Socialist Propaganda 1925–1945.* East Lansing: Michigan State University Press, 1965.

Breithaupt, Hans. *Die Geschichte der 30. Infanterie-Division 1939–1945.* Bad Nauheim: Verlag Hans-Henning Podzun, 1955.

Brett-Smith, Richard. *Hitler's Generals.* San Rafael, Calif.: Presidio Press, 1977.

Calvocoressi, Peter and Guy Wint. *Total War.* New York: Penguin Books, 1979.

Carell, Paul. *Scorched Earth* . Boston: Little, Brown and Co., 1970.

Carroll, Berenice A. *Design for Total War.* The Hague: Mouton and Co., 1968.

Caulaincourt, Armand de. *With Napoleon in Russia.* New York: William Morrow and Co., 1935.

Churchill, Sir Winston. *The Second World War.* 6 vols. Boston: Houghton Mifflin Co., 1950.

Cole, Hugh M. *The Ardennes: Battle of the Bulge.* Washington, D.C.: Department of the Army, 1965.
Conquest, Robert. *The Harvest of Sorrow.* New York: Oxford University Press, 1986.
Cooper, Matthew. *The German Army 1933–1945.* New York: Stein and Day, 1978.
———. *The Nazi War against Soviet Partisans 1941–1944.* New York: Stein and Day, 1979.
Craig, William. *Enemy at the Gates.* New York: E. P. Dutton, 1973.
Creveld, Martin van. *Supplying War.* New York: Cambridge University Press, 1980.
———. *Fighting Power.* Westport, Conn.: Greenwood Press, 1982.
Dallin, Alexander. *German Rule in Russia 1941–1945.* 2d ed. Boulder: Westview Press, 1981.
Deist, Wilhelm. *The Wehrmacht and German Rearmament.* London: The Macmillan Press, 1981.
———, ed. *The German Military in the Age of Total War.* Dover, N.H.: Berg Publishers, 1985.
Department of the Army, Pamphlet #20-234. *Operations of Encircled Forces.* Washington, D.C.: Department of the Army, 1952.
Derry, T. K. *The Campaign in Norway.* London: Her Majesty's Stationary Office, 1952.
D'Este, Carlo. *Decision in Normandy.* New York: E. P. Dutton, 1983.
———. *Bitter Victory.* New York: E. P. Dutton, 1988.
DiNardo, R. L. and Austin Bay. "Horse-Drawn Transport in the German Army." *Journal of Contemporary History* 23, no. 1 (January 1988): 129–42.
Doughty, Robert Allan. *The Breaking Point.* Hamden, Conn.: Archon Books, 1990.
Dower, John W. *War without Mercy.* New York: Pantheon Books, 1986.
Eisenhower, Dwight D. *Crusade in Europe.* New York: Garden City Books, 1951.
Erickson, John. *The Soviet High Command.* New York: St. Martin's Press, 1962.
———. *The Road to Stalingrad.* New York: Harper and Row, 1975.
———. *The Road to Berlin.* Boulder: Westview Press, 1983.
Eurollydon [pseud.]. "The Psychology of the German Regimental Officer." *Royal United Service Institution Journal.* Vol. 82, no. 528 (November 1937): 772–77.
Federal Republic of Germany. *Statistisches Jahrbuch Uber Ernähung—Landwirtschaft und Forsten der Bundesrepublik Deutschland.* Münster-Hiltrup: Landwirtschaftsverlag Gmb.H., 1985.
Fest, Joachim C. *Hitler.* New York: Vintage Books, 1975.
Fugate, Bryan I. *Operation Barbarossa.* Novato, Calif.: Presidio Press, 1984.
Fuller, J.F.C. *On Future Warfare.* London: Sifton Praed and Co., 1928.
Gareis, Martin. *Kampfe und Ende der Fränkisch-Sudetendeutschen 98. Infanterie-Division.* Bad Nauheim: Verlag Hans-Henning Podzun, 1956.
German Army. *Command and Combat of the Combined Arms.* Leavenworth, Tex.: The General Service School Press, 1925.
———. *Pferdeersatzvorschrift.* n.p. 30 September 1936.

Goralski, Robert and Russell W. Freeburg. *Oil and War.* New York: William Morrow and Co., 1987.

Görlitz, Walter. *History of the German General Staff* New York: Praeger Publishers, 1953.

———. *Paulus and Stalingrad.* 1963. Reprint. Westport, Conn.: Greenwood Press, 1974.

Griffith, Paddy. *Forward into Battle.* New York: Hippocrene Books, 1981.

Grossmann, Horst. *Geschichte der rheinisch-westfälischen 6. Infanterie-Division 1939–1945.* Bad Nauheim: Verlag Hans-Henning Podzun, 1958.

Guderian, Heinz. "Heereskavallerie und motorisierte Verbände." *Militär Wochenblatt.* Vol. 119, no. 34 (11 March 1935): 1338-39.

———. "Kraftfahrtruppen." *Militärwissenschaftliche Rundschau* 1, no. 1 (December 1935): 52–78.

———. "Schnell Truppen einst und jetzt." *Militärwissenschaftliche Rundschau* 4, no. 2 (March 1939): 229–43.

———. *Panzer Leader* 1952. Reprint. Washington, D.C.: Zenger Publishing Co., 1979.

Halder, Franz. *The Halder Diaries.* 7 vols. Washington, D.C.: U.S. Army, 1950.

Hardach, Gerd. *The First World War 1914–1918.* Berkeley: University of California Press, 1981.

Harrison, Gordon A. *Cross-Channel Attack.* Washington, D.C.: Department of the Army, 1951.

Haswell, Jock. *The First Respectable Spy.* London: Hamish Hamilton, 1969.

Haupt, Werner. *Heeresgruppe Mitte.* Dorheim: Verlag Hans-Henning Podzun, 1968.

———. *Die 260. Infanterie-Division 1939–1944.* Dorheim: Verlag Hans-Henning Podzun, 1970.

———. *Die Schlachten der Heeresgruppe Süp.* Darmstadt: Podzun-Pallas-Verlag, 1985.

Herzstein, Robert Edwin. *The War That Hitler Won.* New York: Paragon House Publishers, 1987.

Higgins, Trumbull. *Hitler and Russia.* New York: Macmillan Co., 1966.

Hinze, Rolf. *Der Zusammenbruch der Heeresgruppe Mitte im Osten 1944.* Stuttgart: Motorbuch Verlag, 1980.

Hitler, Adolf. *Hitler's Secret Conversations 1941–1944.* New York: Farrar, Strauss and Young, 1953.

———. *Mein Kampf 1943* . Reprint. Boston: Houghton Mifflin Co., 1971.

Hoth, Hermann. *Panzer-Operationen.* Heidelberg: Kurt Vowinckel Verlag, 1956.

Hubatsch, Walther. *61. Infanterie-Division.* Kiel: Verlag Hans-Henning Podzun, 1952.

———. *Weserübung.* Göttingen: Musterschmidt-Verlag, 1960.

Hyams, Jay. *War Movies.* New York: Gallery Books, 1984.

Jacobsen, Hans-Adolf and Jürgen Rohwer, eds. *Decisive Battles of World War II: The German View.* New York: G. P. Putnam's Sons, 1965.

Kardel, Hennecke. *Die Geschichte der 170. Infanterie-Division 1939–1945.* Bad Neuheim: Verlag Hans-Henning Podzun, 1953.

Keilig, Wolf. *Das Deutsche Heer 1939–1945*. 3 vols. Bad Neuheim: Podzun Verlag, 1953.

Kershaw, Ian. *The Hitler Myth*. New York: Oxford University Press, 1987.

Klee, Karl. *Das Unternehmen Seelöwe*. Göttingen: Musterschmidt-Verlag, 1958.

Klein, Burton H. *Germany's Economic Preparations for War*. Cambridge, Mass.: Harvard University Press, 1959.

Klink, Ernst. *Das Gesetz des Handelns: Die Operation "Zitadelle" 1943*. Stuttgart: Deutsche Verlags-Anstalt, 1966.

Koch, H. W. *The Hitler Youth*. New York: Stein and Day, 1976.

Koppes, Clayton R., and Gregory D. Black. *Hollywood Goes to War*. New York: The Free Press, 1987.

Lewis, S. J. *Forgotten Legions*. New York: Praeger Publishers, 1985.

Liddell-Hart, B. H. *The German Generals Talk*. New York: William Morrow and Co., 1948.

———, ed. *The Rommel Papers*. New York: Harcourt, Brace and Co., 1953.

———. *History of the Second World War*. New York: Capricorn Books, 1972.

Lochner, Louis P., ed. *The Goebbels Diaries 1942–1943*. New York: Doubleday and Co., 1948.

Lohse, Gerhart. *Geschichte der rheinisch-westfallischen 126. Infanterie-Division 1940–1945*. Bad Nauheim: Verlag Hans-Henning Podzun, 1957.

Lucas, James. *War on the Eastern Front 1941–1945*. New York: Bonanza Books, 1982.

Luck, Hans von. *Panzer Commander*. New York: Praeger Publishers, 1989.

MacDonald, Charles B. *The Battle of the Huertgen Forest*. New York: Jove Books, 1963.

———. *A Time for Trumpets*. New York: William Morrow and Co., 1985.

———. *The Mighty Endeavor*. 1969. Reprint. New York: William Morrow and Co., 1986.

Mackesy, Piers. "Problems of Amphibious Power: Britain Against France 1793–1815." *Naval War College Review* 30, no. 4 (Spring 1978): 16–25.

Macksey, Kenneth. *Guderian: Panzer General*. London: Macdonald and Jane's, 1975.

Manchester, William. *American Caesar*. New York: Dell Publishing Co., 1978.

Manstein, Erich von. *Aus einem Soldatenleben 1887–1939*. Bonn: Athenäum Verlag, 1958.

———. *Lost Victories*. 1958. Reprint. Novato, Calif.: Presidio Press, 1982.

Mastny, Vojtech. *The Czechs under Nazi Rule*. New York: Columbia University Press, 1971.

Mellenthin, F. W. von. *Panzer Battles*. New York: Ballantine Books, 1971.

Militärgeschichtlichen Forschungsamt. *Das Deutsche Reich und der Zweite Weltkrieg*. 5 vols. Stuttgart: Deutsche Verlags-Anstalt, 1979–89.

Millett, Allan R., and Williamson Murray, eds. *Military Effectiveness*. 3 vols. Boston: Allen and Unwin, 1988.

Milward, Alan S. *The German Economy at War*. London: The Athlone Press, 1965.

Mitcham, Samuel W., Jr. *Hitler's Legions*. New York: Dorset Press, 1985.

Mitchell, Brian R. *European Historical Statistics 1750–1975*. 2d rev. ed. New York: Facts on File, 1981.

Müller, Klaus-Jürgen. *General Ludwig Beck.* Boppard-am-Rhein: Harald Boldt Verlag, 1980.

Müller-Hillebrand, Burkhart. *Das Heer 1933–1945.* 3 Vols., Darmstadt: E. S. Mittler und Sohn Gmb.H., 1954–69.

———.*German Tank Maintenance in World War II.* Washington, D.C.: Department of the Army, 1954.

Murray, Williamson. *The Change in the European Balance of Power 1938–1939.* Princeton: Princeton University Press, 1984.

———. *Luftwaffe.* Baltimore: The Nautical and Aviation Publishing Company of America, 1985.

Nehring, Walter. *Die Geschichte der deutschen Panzerwaffe 1916 bis 1945.* Berlin: Propyläen Verlag, 1969.

Netherlands Central Bureau of Statistics. *Historical Series of the Netherlands 1899–1984.* The Hague: The Netherlands Central Bureau of Statistics, 1985.

Nove, Alec. *An Economic History of the USSR.* New York: Penguin Books, 1969.

Ose, Dieter. *Entscheidung im Westen 1944.* Stuttgart: Deutsche Verlags-Anstalt, 1982.

———. "Rommel and Rundstedt: The 1944 Panzer Controversy." *Military Affairs* 50, no. 1 (January 1986): 7–11.

Overy, R. J. *Göring: The "Iron Man".* London: Routledge and Keegan Paul, 1984.

Paret, Peter, ed. *Makers of Modern Strategy.* Princeton: Princeton University Press, 1986.

Pearton, Maurice. *Oil and the Romanian State.* New York: Oxford University Press, 1971.

Piekalkiewicz, Janusz. *The Cavalry of World War II.* London: Orbis Publishing, 1979.

Pitt, Barrie. *The Crucible of War: Western Desert 1941.* London: Jonathan Cape, 1980.

Poseck, Maximilian von. "Die Kavallerie im Manöver 1930." *Militär Wochenblatt* 115, no. 21 (4 December 1930): 793–97.

———. "Kavallerie von einst und jetzt." *Militär Wochenblatt* 118, no. 43 (18 May 1934): 1464–68.

———. "Aus grosser Zeit vor zwanzig Jahren. Kreigserfahrungen in der Verwendung moderner Kavallerie." *Militär Wochenblatt* 119, no. 30 (11 February 1935): 1171–75.

———. "Aus grosser Zeit vor zwanzig Jahren. Kriegserfahrungen in der Verwendung moderner Kavallerie." *Militär Wochenblatt*, 119, no. 31 (18 February 1935): 1211–13.

Reinhardt, Klaus. *Die Wende vor Moskau.* Stuttgart: Deutsche Verlags-Anstalt, 1972.

Rohde, Horst. *Das Deutsche Wehrmachttransportwesen im Zweiten Weltkrieg.* Stuttgart: Deutsche Verlags-Anstalt, 1971.

Ross, William F. and Charles F. Romanus. *The Quartermaster Corps: Operations in the War against Germany.* Washington, D.C.: Department of the Army, 1965.

Rotundo, Louis, ed. *Battle for Stalingrad.* New York: Pergamon-Brassey's, 1989.

Sajer, Guy. *The Forgotten Soldier*. New York: Ballantine Books, 1972.

Seaton, Albert. *The Russo-German War 1941–45*. New York: Praeger Publishers, 1970.

———. *The German Army 1933–45*. New York: St. Martin's Press, 1982.

Senger und Etterlin, Fridolin von Jr. *Die Panzergrenadiere*. Munich: J. F. Lehmanns Verlag, 1961.

———. *Die 24. Panzer-Division vormals 1. Kavallerie-Division 1939–1945*. Neckargemund: Kurt Vowinckel Verlag, 1962.

———. *Neither Fear nor Hope*. New York: E. P. Dutton, 1964.

Shepperd, G. A. *The Italian Campaign 1943–45*. London: Arthur Barker, 1968.

Short, K.R.M. and Stephan Dolezel, eds. *Hitler's Fall: The Newsreel Witness*. New York: Croon Helm, 1988.

Simpson, George Gaylord. *Horses*. New York: Oxford University Press, 1951.

Speer, Albert. *Inside the Third Reich*. New York: Macmillan Co., 1970.

Stein, George H. *The Waffen SS*. Ithaca, N.Y.: Cornell University Press, 1966.

Steinert, Marlis G. *Hitler's War and the Germans*. Athens: Ohio University Press, 1977.

Stone, Norman. *The Eastern Front 1914–1917*. New York: Charles Scribner's Sons, 1975.

Stoves, Rolf. *Die 1. Panzer Division*. Bad Neuheim: Podzun Verlag, 1961.

Strik-Strikfeldt, Wilfried. *Against Stalin and Hitler*. New York: The John Day Company, 1973.

Taylor, A.J.P. *English History 1914–1945*. Oxford: Oxford University Press, 1965.

Tessin, Georg. *Verbände und Truppen der deutschen Wehrmacht und Waffen SS 1939–1945*. 14 vols. Osnabrück: Biblio Verlag, 1977.

Thorwald, Jürgen. *The Illusion*. New York: Harcourt Brace Jovanovich, 1975.

Tieke, Wilhelm. *Der Kaukasus und das Ol*. Osnabrück: Munin Verlag Gmb.H., 1970.

Trevor-Roper, Hugh R. *Hitler's War Directives 1939–1945*. London: Sidgwick and Jackson, 1964.

Unsigned. "Das Pferd in Heer und Wirtschaft von heute." *Militär Wochenblatt* 121, no. 41 (23 April 1937): 2537–40.

U.S. Department of Agriculture. *Special Report on Diseases of the Horse*. Rev. ed. Washington, D.C.: Government Printing Office, 1942.

U.S. Strategic Bombing Survey (USSBS). "The Effects of Strategic Bombing on the German War Economy." Washington, D.C., 31 October 1945.

———. "German Motor Vehicle Industry Report." January 1947.

Wagener, Carl. *Heeresgruppe Stüd*. Bad Neuheim: Podzun Verlag, 1967.

Wagenführ, Rolf. *Die deutsche Industrie im Kriege 1939–1945*. Berlin: Deutsches Institut für Wirtschaftsforschung, 1955.

Wagner, Hans. "Gedanken über Kampfwagenabwehr." *Militär Wochenblatt* 113, no. 1 (4 July 1928): 10–12.

Wallach, Jehuda L. *The Dogma of the Battle of Annihilation*. Westport, Conn.: Greenwood Press, 1986.

Waring, George H. *Horse Behavior*. Park Ridge, Calif.: Noyes Publications, 1983.

Warmbrunn, Werner. *The Dutch under German Occupation 1940–1945*. Stanford: Stanford University Press, 1963.

Weigley, Russell F. *Eisenhower's Lieutenants*. Bloomington: Indiana University Press, 1981.

Weingartner, James. *Crossroads of Death*. Berkeley: University of California Press, 1979.

Westphal, Sigfried. *The German Army in the West*. London: Cassel and Co., 1951.

Whaley, Barton. *Covert German Reearmament 1919–1939: Deception and Misperception*. Frederick, Md.: University Publications of America, 1984.

Williams, Maurice. "German Imperialism and Austria, 1938." *Journal of Contemporary History* 14, no. 1 (January 1979): 139–53.

Wright, Gordon. *France in Modern Times*. 3d ed. New York: W. W. Norton and Co., 1981.

Zaloga, Steven and Victor Madej. *The Polish Campaign 1939*. New York: Hippocrene Books, 1985.

Ziemke, Earl F. *Stalingrad to Berlin: The German Defeat in the East*. Washington, D.C.: U.S. Army, 1968.

Ziemke, Earl F. and Magna E. Bauer. *Moscow to Stalingrad: Decision in the East*. Washington: U.S. Army, 1987.

Zydowitz, Kurt von. *Die Geschichte der 58. Infanterie-Division 1939–1945*. Kiel: Verlag Hans-Henning Podzun, 1952.

About the Author

R. L. DiNardo is Assistant Professor of History at St. Peter,s College. He is the author of numerous articles on military history in scholarly journals, including *Strategy and Tactics, Journal of Contemporary History,* and *Military Affairs.*

Index

Page numbers in italics indicates illustrations.

Stackpole Military History Series

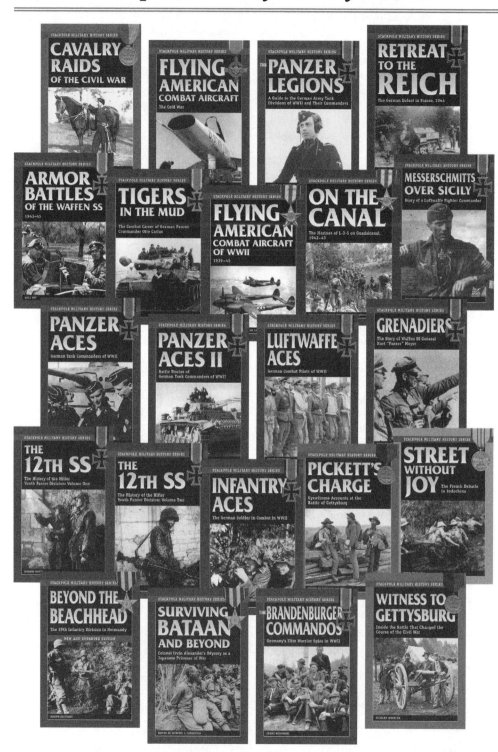

Real battles. Real soldiers. Real stories.

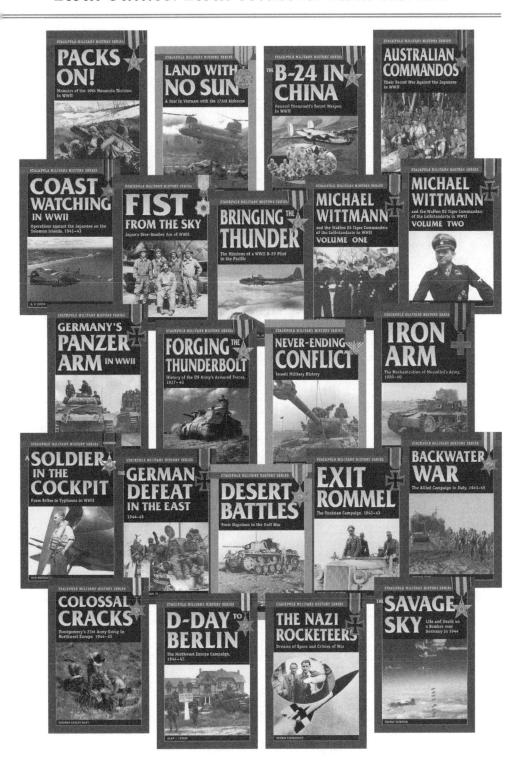

Stackpole Military History Series

Real battles. Real soldiers. Real stories.

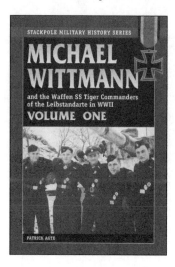

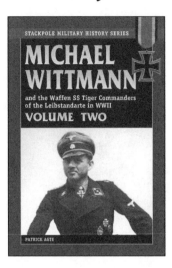

Stackpole Military History Series

ARMOR BATTLES
OF THE WAFFEN-SS
1943–45

Will Fey, translated by Henri Henschler

The Waffen-SS were considered the elite of the
German armed forces in the Second World War and
were involved in almost continuous combat. From
the sweeping tank battle of Kursk on the Russian
front to the bitter fighting among the hedgerows
of Normandy and the offensive in the Ardennes,
these men and their tanks made history.

$19.95 • Paperback • 6 x 9 • 384 pages
32 photos • 15 drawings • 4 maps

WWW.STACKPOLEBOOKS.COM
1-800-732-3669

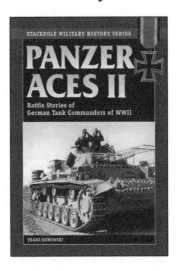

Stackpole Military History Series

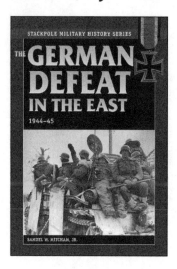

THE GERMAN DEFEAT IN THE EAST
1944–45
Samuel W. Mitcham, Jr.

The last place a German soldier wanted to be in 1944 was the Eastern Front. That summer, Stalin hurled millions of men and thousands of tanks and planes against German forces across a broad front. In a series of massive, devastating battles, the Red Army decimated Hitler's Army Group Center in Belorussia, annihilated Army Group South in the Ukraine, and inflicted crushing casualties while taking Rumania and Hungary. By the time Budapest fell to the Soviets in February 1945, the German Army had been slaughtered—and the Third Reich was in its death throes.

$19.95 • Paperback • 6 x 9 • 336 pages • 35 photos • 21 maps

 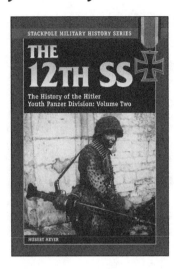

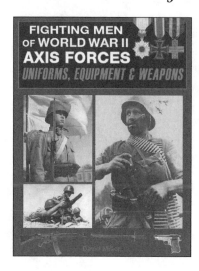